365天的加持
365 Days of Blessings

by

Khenpo Tamgrin Rinpoche

达真堪布仁波切　著

Sūnyatā

書名：365天的加持
系列：心一堂彭措佛緣叢書
　　　達真堪布仁波切譯著文集
作者：達真堪布仁波切

出版：心一堂有限公司
地址：香港九龍尖沙咀東麼地道六十三
　　　號好時中心LG61
電話號碼：(852) 6715-0840
網址：www.sunyata.cc
　　　publish.sunyata.cc
電郵：sunyatabook@gmail.com
心一堂讀者論壇：http://bbs.sunyata.cc
網上書店：http://book.sunyata.cc

香港發行：香港聯合書刊物流有限公司
香港新界大埔汀麗路36號中華商務印刷
大廈3樓
電話號碼：(852)2150-2100
傳真號碼：(852)2407-3062
電郵：info@suplogistics.com.hk

台灣發行：秀威資訊科技股份有限公司
地址：台灣台北市內湖區瑞光路七十六巷
　　　六十五號一樓
電話號碼：+886-2-2796-3638
傳真號碼：+886-2-2796-1377
網絡書店：www.bodbooks.com.tw
心一堂台灣國家書店讀者服務中心：
地址：台灣台北市中山區二0九號1樓
電話號碼：+886-2-2518-0207
傳真號碼：+886-2-2518-0778
網址：www.govbooks.com.tw

中國大陸發行 零售：心一堂
深圳流通處：中國深圳羅湖立新路六號東門
　　　　　　博雅負一層零零八號
電話號碼：(86)0755-82224934
北京：中國北京東城區雍和宮大街四十號
心一堂官方淘寶流通處：
http://sunyatacc.taobao.com/

版次：2015年11月初版

　　　HKD 138
定價：NT　580

國際書號　978-988-8316-56-4

Title: 365 Days Of Blessings
Series: Sunyata Buddhism Series
By KhenpoTamgrin Rinpoche

Published in Hong Kong by Sunyata Ltd
Address: LG61, Houston Center,
63 Mody Road, Kowloon, Hong Kong
Tel: (852) 6715-0840
Website: publish.sunyata.cc
Email: sunyatabook@fmail.com
Online bookstore: http://book.sunyata.cc

Distributed in Hong Kong by:
SUP PUBLISHING LOGISTICS(HK)
LIMITED
Address： 3/F, C & C Buliding,
36 Ting Lai Road, Tai Po, N.T.,
Hong Kong
Tel： (852) 2150-2100
Fax： (852) 2407-3062
E-mail： info@suplogistics.com.hk

Distributed in Taiwan by:
Showwe Information Co. Ltd.
Address: 1/F, No.65, Lane 76, Rueiguang
Road, Neihu District, Taipei, Taiwan
Website: www.bodbooks.com.tw

First Edition 2015

HKD 138
NT 580

ISBN: 978-988-8316-56-4

目錄 *Table of Contents*

365 Days Of Blessings

365天的加持

達真堪布仁波切
Khenpo Tamgrin Rinpoche

一九七三年藏曆八月十五吉祥之日，達真堪布仁波切誕生在四川阿壩的一個佛教世家，父母都是品性善良的佛法修持者。仁波切在充滿著慈悲、仁愛的家庭氛圍中長大，自幼就表現出非同常人的聰慧和深厚善根，幾歲時就有著強烈的出家意願。

On the auspicious day of 15th, the eighth month of Tibetan calendar, 1973, Khenpo Tamgrin Rinpoche was born in a Buddhist family in Abha county, Sichuan Province. His parents are Dharma practitioners of integrity. Grown up in the merciful and kind atmosphere, Rinpoche was excellent by his unordinary faculty and good roots, and expressed the strong will to become a monk when he was little.

 *365 Days Of Blessings*

仁波切七歲時，終於獲得父母同意，如願出家。仁波切出家後，依止當地寺院著名的毛爾蓋克倉、根秋饒吉等活佛為師，潛心學習顯密二乘基礎教理和文化課程。仁波切一貫謙恭謹慎，勤學不倦，悟性甚高，十幾歲時便能輔導《大圓滿前行引導文》、《入菩薩行論》等經論續部，並逐漸承擔寺內許多事務，主持各種法會。

When Rinpoche was seven, he obtained the permission of parents and became a monk. He took refuge in the famous Lama Mudge Khetshangs Rinpoche and Lama Konranurs. After ordained as a monk, he devoted himself to the study of Sutra and Tantra fundamental theories and general knowledge courses. With his sharp faculty, Rinpoche was modest, prudent, and diligent consistently. As a teenager, he helped to teach the Sutra and Tantra such as "The Words of My Perfect Teacher", "The Guide to the Bodhisattvas Way of Life", and began to take charges of many internal affairs in the Monastery and host various assemblies.

365天的加持

十九歲那年，宿世的緣份成熟，仁波切依止了根本上師晉美彭措法王，在色達喇榮五明佛學院，系統修習了五部大論、密宗四續部等顯密教典及諸明處一切經論，接受了大圓滿法的完整傳承和殊勝灌頂。

在法王眾弟子中，仁波切年齡比較小，艱苦的環境愈發能夠考驗他的身心。但仁波切憑著對上師三寶無比具足的信心和頑強、堅韌的毅

In 19 years old, when causes and conditions from previous lives matured, Rinpoche took refuge in his root guru, His Holiness Choeje (Dharma King) Jigme Phuntsok Rinpoche and studied in Larung Gar Buddhist Academy. Systematically, he studied The "Five Great Mahayana treatises, four sections of Tantra, and five sciences (Pañcavidyā), etc. He received the complete lineage and supreme empowerment of DzogChen (Great Perfection) as well.

Rinpoche was relatively young among disciples of the Dharma King. Difficult environment could test his body and mind, he past them continually by holding incomparable faith to the Guru and the Three Jewels

 *365 Days Of Blessings*

力，博覽經卷，慎思明辯，不斷通過各種極其嚴格的考試。二十六歲那年，他以突出的表現、優異的成績和真修實證，獲得了晉美彭措法王親自頒發的五明佛學院最高的堪布學位證書。

堪布原本在佛學院教學部裏承擔教學任務，但在寺院僧眾多次強烈地祈請下，回到朗措瑪寺，坐床法臺，並擔任寺院管委會主任。

and tenacious perseverance. He was well-read, reflected carefully and discriminated clearly. He passed all kinds of strict exams. When he was 26, for his outstanding behavior, excellent scores, and genuine practice and achievement, he obtained the degree of Khenpo, which is the highest degree in Larung Gar Buddhist Academy and awarded by His Holiness Choeje Jigme Phuntsok Rinpoche in person.

Originally, Khenpo was responsible for teaching in Buddhist Academy. Because of the strong request from the sangha of Namstsok Serder Monastery, Khenpo went back, enthroned and took the chair of the Management Association.

2003年，為了給寺院籌集建設資金，堪布來到漢地，發現漢地居士雖然渴求佛法但非常盲目，缺乏善知識的引導，沒有正確、完整的修持方法，因而困於盲修瞎煉的狀態，甚至在拿佛法造業，後果不堪設想。藏地的許多高僧大德即使有心弘揚佛法，但是受制於語言障礙，無法真正利益到他們。

為強烈的悲湣之心和責任感所驅使，堪布發願盡快學成漢

In 2003, in order to raise fund for the construction of monastery, Khenpo came to the Han region , he found that many lay Buddhists had strong desire for Dharma but unfortunately their faith was blind. They lacked qualified teachers' guiding as well as correct and comprehensive way of practicing. They stuck in wrong way of practicing, some even creating bad karma because of applying Buddhism Dharma wrongly. The result would be disastrous. There are many Rinpoches and good Buddhist practitioners from Tibet who wish to preach Buddhism Dharma; they could not really benefit the Han people due to the language limit.

 *365 Days Of Blessings*

語，勢必實現法王如意寶廣度漢地眾生的偉大心願！清淨的發心和堅定的願力不可思議，在上師三寶無比的加持下，通過頑強、不懈的努力，堪布不久就開始用漢語講法，傳授與末法時期眾生相應的殊勝解脫方法——即身成佛的大圓滿和臨終往生的淨土法。

自2005年始，堪布采用網絡與實地相結合的方式弘法。網絡共修平臺包括大圓滿法網站、大圓滿網

Driven by the powerful compassion and sense of responsibility, Khenpo aroused the vows to master Chinese language as soon as possible, and make the Dharma King's wish that salvage the Han people extensively come true definitely. The pure vows and the wishes with strong determination are incredible, with the blessing given by the Guru and the Three Jewels, through his tenacious, untiring efforts, Khenpo began preaching in Chinese very soon the supreme Dharma for liberation which is suitable for the people in the Dharma-ending Age-Dzogchen (The Great Perfection), which enables people to attain Buddhahood in one lifetime, and the Dharma of

絡、共修講堂、大圓滿網絡學院、大圓滿QQ學修群、微信平臺、上師微博、上師博客等。

　　2009年始，堪布在朗措瑪寺兩側修建大圓滿實修中心和十明佛學院。

　　實修中心建好之後，又組建了漢眾僧團及首個漢僧供養團。堪布為促進弟子們的學修，每年還舉辦百日共修、四大法會和佛學夏令營等。十年來，著書幾十冊，匯編為『雪域寶

Pure land which enables people to go to Pure Land when he approaches his end.

From 2005, Khenpo began his teaching by combining internet and face to-face practice. The internet group practice platform including the Great Perfection website, Great Perfection network, Group practice lecture Room, Great Perfection online college, Great Perfection QQ group, WECHAT platform, Guru's Weibo, Guru's blogs, etc.

From 2009, Khenpo started the construction on both sides of Namstsok Serder Monastery, Dzogchen Practice Centre and Ten Sciences Buddhist Institute.

 *365 Days Of Blessings*

藏』、『無上寶藏』和『顯密寶藏』三寶藏。目前，數百個大圓滿實修小組遍布各地，傳承祖師和法王將郎舞弘往漢地以及世界的心願亦在逐漸實現。堪布創建了『達真慈善』事業，積極促進『到達真諦、送達真愛』的佛陀慈悲情懷，逐步成就讓正法弘遍法界的宏圖大願。

堪布之所以能夠受到弟子們的虔敬擁戴，還有一個重要因素，就是他的講法極

After the practice center was built, he organized and found the Han sangha and the first Han nuns Offering Group. To improve disciples' practice, A-hundred-day Group Retreat, four Great Dharma Assemblies and Buddhist summer camp were held every year. In more than ten years, dozens of books had been finished and to be edited as "The Three Treasures" series, including The Snowland Treasures, The Sutra and Tantra Treasures and The Supreme Treasures. Today, hundreds of Dzogchen Practice Groups are scattered everywhere of China. The wish made by lineage patriarchs and the Dharma King to promote Lang Dancing to Han region then around the world is becoming true steadily.

365天的加持

具特色，富有時代的氣息。精妙的思維、睿智的言辭、入心的勸導時時發人深省，驚悟沉迷。他強調夯實加行基礎，按次第學修，在生活與工作中去實實在在地踐行佛法。每個詞、每個字都是那麼地扣人心弦，語言精煉、平易，句句都是修行的竅訣，言簡意賅，特別適合漢地的居士們。很多人因此而發生了翻天覆地的巨大改變，相續與佛法越來越相應，甚至有的

Khenpo founded the "Tamgrin Charity" which advocates the compassionate idea of "to reach the truth, to convey the love". The Great Vow of Preaching the Great Perfection to the whole world is on the way of coming true.

One reason that Khenpo can get devoted and popular support from disciples, is his unique way of modern, subtle, witty and warm teaching. His advices make people contemplate and sober. Emphasizing the preliminary practice, following the sequences, practicing Dharma in life and work honestly, his every word is touching, simple; every sentence is a knack which is easy but meaningful, especially suit the

 *365 Days Of Blessings*

弟子才依止上師仁波切半年，修行就有了極大的成就。

　　縱觀堪布的十年弘法歷程，沒有依賴任何寺院等背景，沒有運用任何活佛等名義、頭銜，而是僅憑自己『寧可捨棄身命，絕不捨棄任何一個眾生』的無私大願，還有他清淨的戒律、廣大的智慧、攝受弟子和度化眾生的善巧方便，感召了無數有緣眾生，超越了一切違緣障礙，將法王的法脈延續到了漢

Han Buddhists. Huge changes happened on many Khenpo's disciples, their continuities are becoming better connected with Dharma. Some even had attained great achievements in just half a year after taking refuge in Khenpo Tamgrin Rinpoche.

Throughout the ten years preaching experiences, Khenpo did not rely on Monastery background or any titles such as Tulku, all he depended on was his great selfless vow that he would rather lose his own life, but would never give up one single being. His pure ethical discipline, extensive wisdom and skillful expedients to teach and guide disciples, moved and inspired countless sentient

365天的加持

地，走向了世界，圓滿了法王的心願。堪布所取得的弘法利生的成就可謂是超前的，功德可謂是無量的。

因由精通顯密的淵博學識、清淨的戒律、無偽的慈悲及廣大的智慧，加之嚴謹簡樸、素食的生活作風，堪布深得僧眾敬仰，德隆望尊，被諸多大德、活佛堪布們一致讚譽並且認為他是一位真正的具德金剛上師。

beings with condition, overcame all hindrances till the Dharma King's lineage came to the Han region and is going towards the world. The wish of the Dharma King is fulfilled. Khenpo's accomplishment of preaching and benefiting sentient beings is incredible, and the merit is immeasurable.

His profound knowledge, pure discipline, sincere compassion and extensive wisdom, his prudent and simple style, as well as being a vegetarian, won sangha's deep respect and great reputation. Many Rinpoches, Tulkus, and Khenpos all praise that Khenpo Tamgrin is an authentic Vajra Guru with full virtues.

 *365 Days Of Blessings*

末法時期的五濁
黑暗愈來愈深重，達
真堪布仁波切弘揚正
法的光芒亦會愈加熾
盛。在上師三寶的加
持、善神護法的護持
下，仁波切利生的宏
願一定會遍亮整個虛
空法界。

In this Dharma-ending Age, the darkness of the Five Turbidities is getting worse, while the radiance of preaching authentic Dharma by Khenpo Tamgrin Rinpoche is becoming brighter. Under the blessing given by the Guru and the Three Jewels, Dharmapala and good deities, the great vow to benefit beings aroused by Rinpoche will shine around the whole dharmadhatu definitely.

365天的加持

發現自己的錯誤，就是開悟；改正自己的錯誤，就是成就。發現了所有的錯誤，就是徹悟；改正了所有的錯誤，就是圓滿。

*I*t is an awakening if you can find your own faults and it is an achievement if you can correct them. It is enlightenment if you can find all of your faults, and it is perfection if you can correct all of them.

因貪嗔癡而產生的一言一行，包括每一個起心動念都是惡；在不貪、不嗔恨、不愚癡的狀態下，一言一行，包括每一個起心動念都是善。

Every word or action, even a thought generated from desire, anger or ignorance is evil. In a state without desire, anger or ignorance, each word or action, including each thought, is virtuous.

多看自己的缺點，才能改正自己的錯誤；多看別人的優點，才能學到別人的功德。

Looking more at your own drawbacks enables you to correct your own faults; looking more at others' strong points enables you to learn others' merits.

你把自己放在最高處時，實際上你在最低處；你把自己放在最低處時，實際上你在最高處。

You are actually at the lowest when you treat yourself as the highest; you are actually at the highest when you put yourself at the lowest.

學佛修行的過程就是懺悔的過程，直至圓滿．成佛的時候才不要懺悔，之前一直都要懺悔。

The process of Dharma practicing is a process of repenting. Before getting perfection and achieving Buddhahood, everybody needs to keep on repenting.

我們都不願意感受痛苦，但是所做的一切都是痛苦的因；我們都想得到快樂，但是所做的一切都不是快樂的因。我們所想與所行都是背道而馳的，這叫顛倒。

All of us are unwilling to suffer but all we have done are the causes of suffering; all of us are willing to be happy but all we have done are not the causes of happiness. Our actions run against our intention, which is called perversion.

365天的加持

觀想不是着相。不執着空，也不執着相，叫不着相。相不是障礙，執着才是障礙。

Visualization is not an attachment to marks. Neither attach to emptiness nor attach to appearance, and this is called detachment to marks. Appearance is not the obstacle but attachment is.

念佛一定能管用，一定能往生，但是我們嘴裡念的是佛，心裡念的是魔，心裡都是私心雜念。這樣「念佛」實際上就是念魔，表面上修行，實際上造業。

Chanting the Buddha's name will definitely work and take you to Pure Land. However, we are just verbally chanting the Buddha's name while our mind is on Mara and is full of selfishness. Such "chanting Buddha" is indeed chanting Mara. It is only a practice in form but karma creation in fact.

365天的加持

讓眾生高興是善事；讓父母高興是孝順。

To satisfy sentient beings is good deed, and to satisfy parents is filial piety.

精進不是一種刻意、一種勉強，而是內心裡的一種歡喜、一種迫切，渴望能學、能修、能得到，而且每時每刻都不忘掉。

Diligence is not a kind of deliberation or reluctance, but a joy and keenness arising from the heart, an eagerness to learn, to practice and to get, and will never be forgotten at all times.

沒有希求正法的心，就沒有意樂圓滿；沒有意樂圓滿，就不能修持正法；不能修持正法，就不能解脫，不能成佛。

Without an eager mind for the true Dharma, there will not be the advantage of intention. One will not be able to practice Dharma without such advantage of intention. No liberation or Buddhahood could be attained without practicing Dharma.

我們是修大乘佛法的，要饒益眾生，但是首先要饒益自己身邊的、與自己最有緣分的眾生。

We should benefit all sentient beings because we are Mahayana (Great vehicle) practitioners, but we should start from the beings around us and most connected to us.

很多人學佛精進不起來，根本原因就是出離心沒有修好。凹外加行是修出離心的方法，把四外加行修好了，相續中才能產生真正的出離心。

Many people are not diligent while practicing Dharma, the basic reason is that they have not aroused the renunciation. The Four Outer Preliminaries are the ways to practice renunciation. The authentic renunciation only arises when the Four Outer Preliminaries are perfectly completed.

 *365 Days Of Blessings*

我們現在所遭受到的所有的痛苦與煩惱，都是來自於對輪迴的貪戀，對世間瑣事的貪着。

All the pains and afflictions we are suffering now come from the clinging to samsara and the attachment to worldly activities.

任何時候都敢面對、敢承担，叫出離心，這是一種勇敢的心；會面對、會承担，叫菩提心，這是一種智慧。

Daring to confront anything and to take the responsibility is called renunciation, which is a brave mind. Knowing well on how to confront and how to take the responsibility is called bodhichitta, which is a kind of wisdom.

修行的過程就是修正自己的過程，不是修正別人的過程。

The process of practicing is to correct self, rather than to correct others.

365天的加持

做自己喜歡做的
事情，不可能
不抓緊。如果不抓緊
時間，學佛修行的事
情一拖再拖，這就說
明了你沒有希求正法
的心，你沒有意樂圓
滿。

You won't postpone for even a second once doing what you are fond of. If you cannot manage your time well and always keep on delaying in practice, it means you have no desideration for true Dharma, nor you have the advantage of intention.

 *365 Days Of Blessings*

福報是修來的,不是求來的。修福報,要具足布施、持戒、忍辱三個條件,如果做不到,不可能得到福報,相反只能減少原有的。

Merits come from practice, rather than entreatment. To practice merits you must have three prerequisites of generosity, precept and forbearance, otherwise you will never obtain merits but the merits you have will also get deducted.

儀軌是方法，通過這種方法才能發心、發願。做任何事情都要有方法，如果方法不正確，做什麼都不會成功。

Rituals are approaches which will inspire the bodhichitta and help us to make vows. Approaches are necessary for doing everything. Wrong approaches lead to failures only.

 *365 Days Of Blessings*

心清淨了，一切都清淨；心自在了，一切都自在。

Once the mind is pure, everything is pure; once the mind is at ease, everything is at ease.

心一動就造業了。不管善業、惡業都是造業，造業就有因果，就要感受果報；有因果就有戲論，有戲論就有輪迴。

Karma is created whenever the mind fluctuates. Karmic acts, no matter good or bad, will bring causes and effects, based on which karmic retribution will be endured. Where there are causes and effects, there is idle theory, and where there is idle theory, there is samsara.

365 Days Of Blessings

受戒是為了讓你增加功德，不是佛要求你什麼，讓你受苦、受累。受戒了就有功德，有功德了就有福報，有福報了就有智慧。

The purpose of receiving precepts is to increase your merits and virtues, rather than to have you suffer hardships and tiredness from what the precept requires. Merits will arise after receiving precepts, with merits there will be fortune, with fortune there will be wisdom.

要認真，但是不能執着；要放下，但是不能放棄。認真是種智慧，執着是種煩惱。不認真是罪過，不執着是解脱。

We should be conscientious rather than be attached. We should cast off but should not give up. Being conscientious is wisdom while being attached is affliction. Not being conscientious is a fault while not being attached is liberation.

365 Days Of Blessings

什麼是真空妙有？不執着是真空，認真是妙有；放下是真空，不放棄是妙有。

What is true emptiness and miraculous existence? Not being attached is true emptiness while being conscientious is miraculous existence; letting go is true emptiness while not giving up is miraculous existence.

一月二十五日　25th, January

我執也是一種貪——貪着自己。

Self-attachment is a kind of desire too-the desire for self.

一月二十六日　　26th, January

真正的佛法就是把握住自己的心，不讓心散亂。心散亂了，活得就痛苦。

The true Dharma is to master your own mind and keep it from being distracted. One will live in pain once the mind is distracted.

365天的加持

一切功德的來源是信心和悲心，一切修法的基礎也是信心和悲心。念念不忘上師三寶，才有堅定的信心；念念不忘父母眾生，才有真正的悲心。

Faith and compassion are the source of all merits as well as the basis of all Dharma practice. Firm faith comes from memorizing the Guru and the Three Jewels constantly while genuine compassion comes from memorizing all parental beings all the time.

人的一生就是一場戲，但是演戲的時候要認真，不能糊塗，不能當真。

Life is just a play, but while performing we should be conscientious, without being confused or taking it to be real.

放下一切眾生叫智慧；不放棄一個眾生叫慈悲。

To let go of all beings is wisdom while not to abandon any being is compassion.

學佛就是學做人——學佛的慈悲，學佛的智慧。

To learn from the Buddha is to learn how to conduct self - We shall learn the Buddha's wisdom as well as the Buddha's compassion.

福報、智慧是每個眾生本來具足的，修福報、修智慧就是讓它顯現出來。你去認識自己，相信自己，承認自己是佛，這叫顯現。

Merits and wisdom are inherent in each being's nature while the practice of the same is to get them manifested. It is called "manifested" when you can understand yourself, trust yourself, and acknowledge yourself being the Buddha.

 *365 Days Of Blessings*

你僅僅放生了不叫行善。從內心裡做一個決定：從今以後全力以赴地愛護一切眾生的生命，這個決心才是行善。

To only free captive animals is not beneficence. Beneficence is a resolution from your mind to cherish all beings' lives with all efforts from then on.

不是將不清淨的東西觀為清淨，將不圓滿的東西觀為圓滿，而是本來就是清淨，就是圓滿。認識到了這個道理，並且證得了這個道理，這叫開悟、證悟。

It is not to view the impure as pure or to view the imperfect as perfect, but everything is pure and perfect by nature. When you have realized and understood such principle, it's called enlightenment.

阿彌陀佛是真心想接我們，關鍵我們是不是真心想去？如果真心想去，肯定會時時刻刻都發這個願，到臨終的時候也不會忘。

Buddha Amitabha sincerely wants us to come, while the key factor is whether we want to go there wholeheartedly? If we really want to go, we will definitely make such aspiration all the time and never forget it until the point of dying.

回向的對境是無量的，功德也是無量的，這是使功德得以圓滿的一種善巧方便。為自己、為某某眾生回向，得到的功德小，因為對境小，心量小。

If the objects of dedication are boundless, the merits so generated are also boundless, and this is an expedient way to complete merits. To dedicate to self or certain being could only generate trivial merits, since the mind is narrow and the objects are limited.

你能解脫，這是上師三寶的一種期望；你能利益眾生，這是上師三寶更大的期望。你為了這些去愛護身體和生命，實際上是愛護諸佛菩薩的事業，愛護父母眾生的利益，不是為自己。

It is the Guru and the Three Jewels' expectation that you could be liberated, and it is their even bigger expectation that you could benefit other beings. To cherish your body and life for such reason is indeed to cherish the saints' undertakings as well as to cherish the parental beings' interests, rather than for self.

365天的加持

看見佛菩薩，看見光了，有各種好的征相和夢境，也是好事，但是這不等於解脫，也不等於成就。任何時候都不起煩惱，沒有痛苦，才是解脫，才是成就。

The sight of the Buddha and Bodhisattva, and the sight of lights or various auspicious signs and dreams are good but are not necessarily equal to getting liberated or accomplished. It is liberation or accomplishment only when you are not arousing afflictions or having pains at all times.

 *365 Days Of Blessings*

火點燃了，灰自然就有。只要去做利益眾生的事情，世間的福報自然而然就來。

*A*sh comes naturally after fire has been lighted-up. As long as you act to benefit others, worldly rewards will come automatically.

有智慧的人，為自己的時候去為眾生，卻使自己得到解脫；沒有智慧的人，為自己的時候就是為自己，卻什麼也得不到。

The wise acts to benefit other beings but he himself gets liberated finally, while the fool acts to benefit himself only and gets nothing in the end.

有善知識的指點，依照他的要求做，這叫會學；有正確的方法，按照正確的方法修，這叫會修。

Having the spiritual friends' guidance and being able to follow their instructions are called be good at learning. Having right methods and following such methods to practice are called be good at practicing.

你最執着的東西對你傷害最大。你對哪件事、哪個人、哪句話執着心最強，它對你的傷害就最大，人就是這麼被傷害的。

What you obsess about the most hurts you the most, no matter it is an event, a person or a sentence, and people are hurt likewise.

根本不知道什麼是佛、什麼是往生、什麼是西方極樂世界，還念佛求往生，這叫迷信。信，要先明理，明理了，才能深信；深信了，才有堅定不移的信心。

Without knowing anything about what is the Buddha, what is rebirth and what is the Western Pure Land of Great Bliss but still reciting Buddha names for taking rebirth is called superstition. One should first understand the doctrine then he can have deep faith. Only with deep faith, can he attain firm and unshakable confidence.

修行不在表面上，在心上，每個起心動念都是修行。真正有修行了，誰也障礙不了你。

Practice is not reflected externally but in the mind, and each thought is practice. With genuine practice, nobody can obstruct you.

我們一定要學佛修行，但是在這個過程中不能捨棄眾生，不能放棄自己的責任和義務。該做的一定要做好，該盡的義務一定要盡到。

We must practice Dharma. However, during the process we shall not abandon other beings nor abdicate our responsibilities and obligations. Whatever to be performed must be performed well and whatever obligation to be fulfilled must be fulfilled without fail.

365天的加持

從心裡做決定：「「我要給予一切眾生安樂」，這是慈心；「我要拔除一切眾生的痛苦」，這是悲心。對每一個眾生都發這樣的心，才是無量的慈悲心。

A resolution made from your mind that "I must give all beings happiness" is kindness, that "I must eradicate all beings' sufferings" is compassion. Only the resolution for EACH being is boundless kindness and compassion.

不追逐快樂，也不執着快樂的時候，快樂自然就來了；不逃避痛苦，也不執着痛苦的時候，痛苦自然就遠離了。佛法的奧妙也正在這裡。

Happiness comes automatically when you are not pursuing or clinging to it, sufferings leave spontaneously when you are not avoiding or attaching to them. The secret of Dharma lies right here.

365天的加持

46

魔，分心魔和外魔，外魔是心魔的顯現，心魔才是真正的魔。

There are demons in mind and demons outside. The demons outside are the manifestation of demons in mind. The demons in mind are the real demons.

二月十七日　17th, February

當我們能夠完全為眾生的時候，才能斷除我執、我愛，才能降伏貪嗔癡慢疑這些煩惱；降伏了這些煩惱，才能不造業；不造業了，才能不受惡果。

Only when we are able to act wholly for other beings can we renounce self-attachment and self-love, and further subdue the afflictions such as desire, hatred, ignorance, arrogance and doubt. Only when we have subdued such afflictions, can we stop creating karma and further avoid enduring bad effects.

365天的加持

我們研究佛法，修持佛法，就是為了增強對上師三寶的信心，對自己的信心，對一切法的真相和真理的信心。修行的過程就是增加信心的過程。

The purpose of studying and practicing Dharma is to increase our confidence in the Guru and the Three Jewels, the confidence in ourselves and the confidence in the truth and reality of all phenomena. The process of the practice is just the process to increase confidence.

 *365 Days Of Blessings*

自己的功德、福慧圓滿了，沒有絲毫的自私自利心，才可以觀察別人，修正別人，之前沒有資格。

Only when your merit, fortune and wisdom are completed and not even a slightest mind of selfish is left, are you allowed to observe and correct others, before then you are not qualified.

不管是富貴還是貧窮，如果你覺着活得累、活得痛苦，這就是命不好；始終無法使自己滿意，達不到自己的願望，這就是運氣不好。

Whether rich or poor, as long as you feel that living is tired and painful, it is an unkind fate; as long as you could never get yourself satisfied or get your wishes fulfilled, it is a bad fortune.

很多人都把佛當神，把佛法當神話，當作承辦世間瑣事的工具，向佛求各種福報。如果你有所求，就不是佛法了。

*M*any treat the Buddha as a deity and treat Dharma as a fairytale as well as means to obtain worldly affairs, thus entreat the Buddha for various interests. Whenever you are pursuing something, it is already not Dharma.

認真是一種緣起的作用，是完全的解脫；執着是輪迴的因，是真正的痛苦。不執着了才有認真，才沒有痛苦。

Conscientiousness is a function of dependent origination and also a complete liberation, while attachment is the cause of samsara and also an actual suffering. Only without attachment can there be conscientiousness and no suffering.

對世間法，對一切法，沒有絲毫的貪着，叫放下；認真地承担起自己的責任和義務，叫不放棄。

When you do not have even a slightest attachment to all mundane laws and all phenomena, it is called letting go. When you conscientiously assume your responsibilities and obligations, it is called not giving up.

自信不是傲慢，是種正見，是對自己的正確認識，對自己的法喜充滿。傲慢是種邪見，是種無明煩惱。

Self-confidence is not arrogance but a right view. It is a right comprehension about self, and bliss of Dharma within self. Arrogance is a wrong view and an affliction of ignorance.

智慧是在人和事當中磨煉出來的。每遇到一次違緣，就能增長一種智慧；每遇到一次障礙，就能提高一個層次。

Wisdom is cultivated through interactions with people and things. Whenever coming across an unfavorable condition, one can grow a kind of wisdom; whenever encountering an obstacle, one can improve to a higher level.

觀察自己的毛病，改正自己的毛病，才是改變命運。毛病越少，命運越好；毛病越多，命運越不好。

The observation of your own mistakes and the correction of such mistakes are "changing the fate". The fewer the mistakes, the better the fate. The more the mistakes, the worse the fate.

如果有我執我愛、自私自利，你怎麼想，也想不到周全和完美；你怎麼做，也做不到圓滿和究竟。

With self-attachment, self-love and selfishness, no matter how you think, you can never come out with completeness and perfectness, and no matter how you act, you can never reach consummation and ultimateness.

隨喜是善心，是正念，它對治了嫉妒、嗔恨心等煩惱，這是最大的善根，最殊勝的正念。好比一滴水雖然微不足道，但是它一旦融入大海中，就擁有了大海的力量。

Accordingly rejoicing is a kindness as well as a right view. It corrects the afflictions of jealousy, hatred and so forth. Hence, it is the greatest virtue and the most supreme right view. Just like a drop of water, although negligible, once entering the sea, it owns the sea's power.

 *365 Days Of Blessings*

我執、我愛，自私自利，貪嗔癡慢疑，是心魔，是真正的魔。

Self-attachment, self-love, selfishness, desire, hatred, ignorance, arrogance and doubt, are all demons in mind, which are the real demons.

不盡責任，不盡義務，是罪過；真正能盡到責任、盡到義務，是修行，是功德。

It is an evil conduct if you do not take your responsibilities or fulfill your obligations; it is practice and merit if you can really complete and fulfill your duty and obligations.

只有放下一切，才能得到一切；不放下，什麼也得不到。

Let go of everything, and you will get everything; otherwise, you will get nothing.

三月四日 *4th, March*

斷習氣，斷煩惱，有一定的過程，不要着急，着急也是一種障礙。

*I*t takes some time to get rid of our bad habitual tendencies and afflictions. So it is not necessary to worry, because worry is also a kind of barrier.

365 Days Of Blessings

佛法是圓融一切
的，你能真正圓
融一切的時候，才有
佛法；佛法是容納一
切的，你能真正容納
一切的時候，才有佛
法。

Dharma combines everything, so only when you are able to combine everything, you have Dharma; Dharma accommodates everything, so when you are able to accommodate everything, you have Dharma.

你的發心動機是惡，你所做的一切都是惡，別人怎麼讚嘆，都沒有用；你的發心動機是善，你所做的一切都是善，別人怎麼誹謗，也沒有事。在上師三寶面前，在因果面前，自己是清白的。

If your motivation is evil, everything you do will be evil, and it will never work however you are praised by others; if your motivation is virtuous, everything you do will be virtuous, and it doesn't matter however you are slandered, because in front of the Guru and the Three Jewels, and in front of causes and effects, you are innocent.

 *365 Days Of Blessings*

你最執着的，是對你傷害最大的，也是最能考驗你的。它傷害你的時候，你能不動心，能放下，才算過關。

What you are obsessed with most seriously will hurt you and test you most badly. Therefore, when it hurts you, you should remain unaffected and let go, then you can conquer it.

佛也演戲，凡夫也演戲，但是佛不執着，不糊塗，佛知道自己在演戲，所以沒有煩惱、痛苦。凡夫就迷在這裡——因為不知道自己在演戲，都當真了，於是煩惱痛苦。

Buddha acts and the ordinary person also acts, but Buddha is neither obsessed nor confused as he knows he is acting so he does not feel the pain and trouble. While the ordinary person feels the opposite way since he does not know he is acting and takes everything to be real.

 *365 Days Of Blessings*

心的變化，是高超魔術師的表演，看起來特別神奇、奧妙，任誰也辨認不出來。但當我們真正明白了，才知道，一點都不複雜，都是它變的。

The change created by the mind is like the performance given by a skilled magician, it looks so magical and subtle that nobody can figure it out. But, when we finally understand it, we will figure out that the change is not complicated at all, since it is all created by our mind.

心裡沒有障礙，就沒有外魔的干擾和侵害。主要是我們的心不清淨，心態不平衡，才產生障礙。

If you do not have doubts and puzzles in your mind, then you won't be interfered or harmed by the evils outside. What causes the doubts and puzzles in your mind is the impurity and imbalance state of your mind.

 *365 Days Of Blessings*

看不見自己的缺點和毛病，只能看見別人的缺點和毛病，這是傲慢心的特點。它是一切痛苦的根源。

One of the characters of arrogance is that one can always point out others' weaknesses and drawbacks while seeing nothing from self, which is the root cause of pain.

365天的加持

我們都在做夢。晚上做的夢是黑夢，白天做的夢是白夢。晚上的夢很容易醒，白天的夢很難醒。醒過來了叫覺，沒有醒過來叫迷。

We are all dreaming. What we do at night is black dream and what we do at daytime is white dream. It is easy to wake up from the black one but not easy to wake up from the white one. The awakened state is "aware" while the un-awakened stated is "deluded".

 *365 Days Of Blessings*

三月十三日　　　　*13th, March*

無常分兩種：一個是粗大相續之無常；一個是細微剎那之無常。剎那無常和空性是一個道理，真正明白了這個道理，才能證悟空性。證悟無常，是證悟空性的因。

Impermanence has two types: one is big and continuous impermanence and the other one is tiny and instant impermanence. The truth of instant impermanence is the same as emptiness, which means if you can understand instant impermanence then you can get the meaning of emptiness. Understanding impermanence is the precondition of understanding emptiness.

365天的加持

舍無量心，是捨棄對親朋好友的貪戀，捨棄對怨敵仇人的怨恨，能平等地對待一切眾生。

The mind of boundless impartiality is to give up the attachment to family and friends, to abandon the hatred against enemies, and to treat all the beings fairly and equally.

365 Days Of Blessings

三月十五日 *15th, March*

面對任何人、任何事、任何境不起煩惱叫看破放下。順境要安心，逆境也要安心，一切境中心如如不動。

When you can refrain from arousing any annoyance no matter whom or what you are facing, you can call it "let-it-go". No matter what situation you are in, good or bad, you need to be easy and calm.

能讓自己快樂、自在，這是真聰明、真能幹；能讓自己和他人解脫煩惱與痛苦，這是真智慧、真慈悲。

If you can make yourself happy and free, you are smart and capable; but if you can make not only you but also others free from the troubles and pains, you are wise and compassionate.

 *365 Days Of Blessings*

看住這個心，叫修禪；把自己的心從執着、妄想的牢獄中解放出來，叫修密。

When you can watch your mind, you are practicing Zen and if you can liberate your mind from attachment and delusion, you are practicing Vajrayana.

三月十八日　　　　18th, March

不傷害眾生，就是
斷惡；不僅不傷
害，而且還能讓他們
高興，利益他們，叫
行善。

*Not harming beings
is renouncing
the evil while bringing
happiness and benefits to
them is doing the virtue.*

365 Days Of Blessings

我們可以享受福報，但是不能浪費福報。浪費自己的時間、財產、功德和一些好的機緣，都是浪費福報。

We can enjoy our blessings but we cannot waste them. Wasting our time, property, merits, virtues and good opportunities is wasting our blessings.

什麼叫法弱魔強？精神世界越來越落後，正知正見越來越弱，叫法弱；物質世界越來越發達，邪知邪見越來越強，叫魔強。

What is the "evil excels Dharma"? When the spiritual world turns poorer and poorer, the right thoughts become weaker and weaker, then it is called weak Dharma; when the material world gets more and more developed, the evil thoughts become stronger and stronger, it is called strong evil.

 *365 Days Of Blessings*

佛法是完全平等自由的，八萬四千法門都是脫離痛苦的方法，你可以根據自己的條件、根基、福報和緣分來選擇。關鍵是，學哪個法門都要認真，修哪個法門都要堅持。

Dharma is totally equal and free. All the 84,000 means are ways for us to get rid of pains and sufferings. You can surely choose one of those according to your condition, level, virtue and fate. However, the key is to practice it wholeheartedly with perseverance.

不懂因果的人，就是不懂佛法的人；不取捨因果的人，就是不修持佛法的人；不相信因果的人，就是不相信佛法的人。

One who doesn't understand causes and effects doesn't know Dharma; one who doesn't know how to treat causes and effects isn't practicing Dharma; one who doesn't believe in causes and effects doesn't believe in Dharma.

我們隨喜他人的功德，就能得到他人所做的功德；如果對他人所做的惡業也有歡喜心，同樣也有罪過。

When we are accordingly rejoicing for others' merit we can also benefit from it; similarly, if we accordingly rejoice for others' evil karma we will have it in return too.

三月二十四日 *24th, March*

每個人的心中都有一片淨土，把清淨心修出來，讓心中的淨土顯現出來，就活着往生了，到淨土了，到西方極樂世界了。

There is a pure land in everybody's mind. If we can have a pure heart and get it manifested then we are already transferred, while still living, to the Western Pure Land of Ultimate Bliss.

你的身體就是壇城，要愛護這個壇城，莊嚴這個壇城，讓眾生生起歡喜心。

Your body is the mandala, so you need to protect it and dignify it, which can bring the happiness for all beings.

你所面對的所有的事情，都是修行的對境。

All the things you are dealing with are the objects of your practice.

你發心、發願為眾生學佛、成佛，按上師的要求盡心盡力地、如理如法地學修，這叫法供養，也叫法布施。這是對上師三寶最大的供養，也是對父母眾生最大的布施。

If you can arouse the determination and aspiration to learn Dharma and to become the Buddha for the benefit of all beings, and meanwhile, if you can try your best to practice properly according to the Guru's requirements, it is called Dharma offering, or Dharma giving. This is the best offering to the Guru and the Three Jewels, as well as the best giving to all beings.

怎樣判斷自已有沒有修行？煩惱、習氣減少了，慈悲心、菩提心增加了，對上師三寶具有堅定不移的信心了，才是真有修行了。

*H*ow do you judge whether you are practicing? If your annoyances and bad habits have decreased, your compassion and bodhichitta have increased, and you have got unshakable faith in your Guru and the Three Jewels, then you are really practicing.

 *365 Days Of Blessings*

讓別人一步,實際上是讓自己一步。

To concede to others is actually to concede to self.

三月三十日 *30th, March*

放下了一切眾生，是大徹大悟；不放棄一個眾生，是人慈大悲。真正明白了這些，叫開悟；真正做到了這些，叫解脫。

Letting go of all beings is thorough realization. Not giving up any being is real compassion. The real understanding of these is enlightenment, and the real achievement of these is liberation.

 *365 Days Of Blessings*

生活圓滿了，工作圓滿了，才是真正的圓滿。如果生活沒有圓滿，工作沒有圓滿，另外得到一個圓滿沒有什麼用。

The completeness of both life and work leads to real completeness. Without the completeness of life or work, to get any other completeness is meaningless.

有無「我」的智慧，才可能有菩提心。如果不能把「我」忘掉，想完全為眾生是很難的，口頭上說說而已。

With the wisdom of "no-self" cognition, one may get *bodhichitta*. With the attachment to "self", it's very hard to wholeheartedly serve all beings. In that case, it's only oral work.

真正有修行的人，見解越高，取捨因果的行為越細。

For a real practitioner, the higher his opinion is, the more careful his action in selecting and rejecting the causes and effects is.

如果你的煩惱、習氣減少了，沒有什麼可追求的，也沒有什麼可放下的，內心真的輕鬆、自在了，就成就了。

If you have fewer annoyances or bad habits than before and have nothing to pursue or cast off, feel relaxed and free, then you are accomplished.

佛已經將脫離痛苦的方法教給我們了，我們按照佛的要求去做，然後再把這個方法告訴他人，也讓他人這樣做，這叫弘揚佛法。

The Buddha has taught us the method to break away from sufferings. If we do according to his teaching, tell the method to others and ask them to follow suit, then we are promoting Dharma.

如果有看不起的人，說明你還沒有慈悲心；如果有看不慣的事，說明你還沒有智慧，修行還沒有到位。

If there are still some people who you look down upon, that means you haven't got compassion; if there are still something that you can't put up with, that means you haven't got wisdom and still need to practice.

 *365 Days Of Blessings*

菩薩眼裡沒有看不起的人，沒有看不慣的事。如果想成佛，先學當菩薩。連菩薩都當不好，不可能成佛。

In the eyes of the Bodhisattva, everyone and everything is perfect. If you want to become the Buddha, first of all, try to learn to become a Bodhisattva. If you can't do as good as a Bodhisattva, it's impossible to become the Buddha.

看別人不順眼，是自己修行不夠，別人的毛病都是你挑出來的，如果不挑哪有毛病呢？

If you don't like others, that means you haven't practiced enough. Just because you are particular about others, you can pick out their faults. Otherwise, how can you find their faults?

有也行，沒有也行；既不追求，也不拒絕。來去都是自然，都是應該。沒有什麼可高興的，也沒有什麼可傷心的，都是演戲。緣來緣去，很正常，已經都看透了，弄明白了，不會為這些動心，這叫如如不動的心。

It doesn't matter whether you have it or not. Neither pursue nor reject. It is destined to get or lose it, so there is no reason to be happy or sad. Everything is just a play. It's normal whether to get or lose it. Since one has outguessed everything, his mind won't get disturbed, which is called unshakable mind.

365天的加持

饒益眾生實際上是饒益自己，所有的功德、福德和善根都是自己的。如果你只想饒益自己，不可能得到真正的利益，因為你的所想和所做是相反的，惡因是永遠不可能得到善果的。

Benefiting others is actually benefiting self, because all the merits, blessings and good roots belong to self. If you just intend to benefit self, you can't get real benefits, because what you think is opposite to what you do, and vicious causes will definitely never get good effects.

眾生是不停地轉輪迴，佛是不停地轉淨土。眾生是因對輪迴的貪戀轉來的；佛是因對眾生的悲心轉來的。

The beings keep transmigrating in samsara while the Buddha keeps transmigrating in pure land. The transmigration of the beings is due to the clinging to samsara while the same of the Buddha is due to the compassion to the beings.

佛讓你對一切都不能執着，不能分別。但是你非去執着上師三寶，然後又分別上師三寶。這樣你還是沒有成就。

The Buddha teaches you not to attach to or discriminate everything. However, you insist on attaching to the Guru and the Three Jewels and discriminate them afterwards. Therefore you are still not accomplished.

 *365 Days Of Blessings*

你學得不好，是剛學的，所以更要認真學。如果總是用這些理由原諒自己，你永遠沒有辦法精進修行，更難以在今生解脫。

"*I am weak in Dharma learning since I am a beginner*", thus you need to practice more seriously. If you always forgive yourself by using such excuses, you will never be able to learn diligently nor will you get liberated in this life.

365天的加持

修持不能等待，因為死亡不會等待。我們學佛、修行，一定要趕在死亡的前面。

We cannot postpone our practice because the death will not wait for us. We must learn and practice Dharma before the death comes.

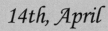

一定要好好地修忍辱。如果不修忍辱，哪怕有一剎那的嗔恨心，也會摧毀一千個大劫積累的福慧資糧。

You must practice patience diligently. Without practicing patience, even a single fit of rage can destroy the merits and wisdom you have accumulated over a thousand kalpas.

很多人形式上學佛、念佛，實際上求名聞利養。不要只看眼前利益，目光放遠一些，少發俗願，多做利益眾生的事。

Many people only learn Dharma and recite Buddha names in form but pursue fame and wealth in fact. Do not merely focus on immediate interests, look at the longer run, make less worldly aspirations, and do more things for the benefit of all beings.

 *365 Days Of Blessings*

活沒有信心，死沒有決心，世間法沒有成就，出世間法也沒有成就，這種人怎麼都不行。能脫離輪迴，擺脫痛苦，解脫成佛，救度更多的眾生，才是真正的人。

No confidence while living, no resolution while dying, no achievement in worldly concerns and no accomplishment in supermundane paths. Those people can accomplish nothing. Only those being able to escape from samsara, break away from sufferings, get liberation and attain Buddhahood so as to save more sentient beings are the genuine human beings.

只念佛、誦經，不顧家，也不顧孩子，讓他們煩惱、痛苦，這也是惱害眾生。

Only chanting sutras and reciting Buddha names while neglecting the family and children even having them suffer pains and annoyance is also a hurt to sentient beings.

有欲望就有失望，有盼望就有絕望。欲望越大，失望越大；盼望越大，絕望越大。

*O*nce there is desire, there is disappointment. Once there is hope, there is desperation. The stronger the desire, the deeper the disappointment. The bigger the hope, the higher the desperation.

放不下的原因就是害怕——害怕離開，害怕失去，害怕得不到。真正弄明白了什麼是放下，那個時候才不會害怕，才能放下。

The reason for not being able to cast off is fear-fear of leaving, fear of losing, fear of not getting. Only when you have really understood what cast-off is, can you get rid of fear and cast everything off.

真正有出離心了，能夠放下了，不用放棄一件事，不用放棄一個人，一切都可以接納。

With true renunciation and being able to cast off, you can accept everything without giving up any person or anything.

365天的加持

佛 法是恆順，佛法
是圓融，佛法是
容納。真正放下了，
才能恆順一切，才能
圓融一切，才能容納
一切。

Dharma is to be agreeable, to combine and to accommodate. Only when you are really able to let go, can you be agreeable to everything, combine everything and accommodate everything.

上師三寶不在別處，在心中。你的恭敬心、誠心、善心、信心，就是佛力的加持，就是上師三寶的加持。心不善、不誠，你怎麼求，怎麼拜，都沒有用。

The Guru and the Three Jewels are nowhere else but in your mind. The mind of reverence, sincerity, kindness and faith is the blessing of Buddha-power as well as the blessing from the Guru and the Three Jewels. Without a kind and sincere mind, it will never work no matter how you entreat or worship the Buddha.

365天的加持

你 的眼淚是為眾生
流的嗎？

A re your tears shed for the beings?

無常面前，不分老少，人人平等。

In front of impermanence, everyone, old or young, is equal.

我們都是凡夫，每天會犯很多戒。犯戒不怕，怕不懺悔，怕不會懺悔。不懺悔就是過失，會懺悔就是修行。

We are all ordinary people and will transgress many precepts every day. However, what is terrible is not the transgression of the precepts, but not to confess or not knowing how to confess. Not to confess is a fault while being able to confess is a practice.

 *365 Days Of Blessings*

講輪迴的過患，都不愛聽，尤其是現在的年輕人。愛聽不愛聽都是這樣。佛講的是道理，不是故事，輪迴確實是這麼苦。

The people, especially the young at present age, do not like to hear the defects of samsara. But it is a fact that no matter whether you like or do not like it, what the Buddha told us is the truth rather than stories. Samsara is really that suffering.

靠緣分找上師，靠根基找法門。選擇一位有緣的上師，選擇一個相應的法門，這不是分別，而是一種修持方法。

Look for the teacher by destiny and look for the Dharma-gate by capacity. To find a right teacher and to choose an appropriate Dharma-gate is a means of practice rather than a kind of discrimination.

365 Days Of Blessings

當你真心實意想學佛、想修行，解脫是最容易、最簡單的事。

Getting liberation is the easiest and simplest thing as long as you want to learn and practice Dharma whole-heartedly.

讓自己的心胸像天空一樣廣闊，像大海一樣寬容，像大山一樣穩定。

Have your mind as broad as the sky, as generous as the sea, and as stable as the mountain.

業力沒有顯現的時候，我們可以轉變因果，可以改變命運；業力現前的時候，像洪水一樣，誰也攔不住。那個時候才相信輪迴的痛苦，已經晚了。

Before karmic power manifests, we can convert our causes and effects and change our fate. Once it comes, similar to a flood, nobody can stop it. It is already late to realize the pain of samsara only at that particular time.

結緣是為了了緣，只有好好地結緣，才能好好地了緣。什麼叫了緣？不管小事、大事，樣樣事都認真、用心去做。小事不嫌棄，大事也不害怕。

Making connections is for ending the destinies. Only to make connections nicely can you end the destinies successfully. What is to end the destinies? It is to do everything, small or big, sincerely and wholeheartedly. Do not avoid the small and do not fear the big.

 *365 Days Of Blessings*

把所有的方便都讓給別人，把所有的困難都留給自己，這是我們的一種最佳修行。

Giving all conveniences to others while leaving all difficulties with self, this is a best way of practice.

如果你的内心還是不輕鬆，不自在，還有煩惱、痛苦，就不叫解脫。

It is not liberation if your mind is not free and easy and you are still having pains and troubles.

你會學佛，才能成佛；如果你不會學佛，永遠不會解脫，不會成佛。

Only when you know how to learn Dharma can you become a Buddha. If you don't know how to learn, you can never get liberation or become a Buddha.

你所謂的敵人、仇人才是你真正的善知識、上師，才是你最大的恩人。他們通過很多方式指出你的毛病，讓你知道自己的缺點，這是最好的竅訣。

The so-called enemy is indeed your genuine virtuous mentor and the Guru, as well as your biggest benefactor. They point out by various means your weaknesses and help you understand your drawbacks, which is the best pith instruction.

 *365 Days Of Blessings*

不可能任何人都喜歡你，也不可能任何人都討厭你；不可能任何人都讚嘆你，也不可能任何人都誹謗你。你只要不動心就行了。

It is impossible that everyone likes you or everyone hates you. It is also impossible that everyone praises you or everyone slanders you. It will be all right as long as your mind remains unmoved.

有正知正見才能對付邪知邪見。沒有邪知邪見，才沒有煩惱；沒有煩惱，才不造業；不造業，才不感受痛苦。

Only with right views are you able to deal with wrong views. Only without wrong view can there be no affliction. Only without affliction can you create no karma and suffeno pains.

慈悲心就是對每一個眾生都一樣：對自己兒女的感情和對一切眾生的感情是一樣的；對自己父母的感恩和對一切眾生的感恩是一樣的。

It is compassion when you can treat each being equally: to love all beings the same as to love your own children; to gratitude all beings the same as to gratitude your own parents.

你好好地表法、表演，才是度化眾生的善巧方便。

Your whole-hearted acts or performance is an expedient way to guide all sentient beings.

沒有平靜的心，就不會有清淨處，也不會有平平安安的事。

Without a calm mind there would be no pure places, nor peaceful things.

整個宇宙都是我的家,所有的眾生都是我的家人。

The whole universe is my home and all sentient beings are my family members.

看一切人都是好人，看一切事都是好事，看一切處都是好處，才是解脫。

It is liberation only when you can view all people as good people, all things as good things and all places as good places.

真正的快樂不是擁有的多，而是計較的少。

The real happiness does not lie in how much you own, but in how little you bother.

把每時每刻都當成自己的臨終。每時每刻都提醒自己：假如這是我的最後時刻……

*T*reat every moment as your point of death and keep reminding yourself: if this is my last minute....

不出家不能真正學佛、修行。這裡說的不是身出家，而是心出家。心出家是指有出離心。

If one can't become a monastic, one can't really study Buddhism and practice. Here it means to become a monastic not physically but mentally, which refers to disenchantment with samsara.

365 Days Of Blessings

什麼是敢面對、敢承担？不管好壞，任何時候都不動心，心不隨境轉，不動搖。

*W*hat does it mean to confront and to take responsibility? Whether it is good or bad, never become disturbed, be influenced by outside surroundings, or change the mind.

世界上沒有什麼完美，想開了，想通了，就是完美。世界上沒有什麼完美，知足了、少欲了，就是完美。世界上沒有什麼完美，隨緣了、放下了，就是完美。

Nothing in the world is perfect, so seeing through and figuring out is perfect. Nothing in the world is perfect, so being content with less desire is perfect. Nothing in the world is perfect, so following causes and effects and casting off is perfect.

 *365 Days Of Blessings*

如果把對生活、對工作的付出用在學佛修行上，你一定能解脫，一定能成佛。

If you apply the efforts that you make in life and work to studying Buddhism, you are bound to be liberated and to become the Buddha.

你真正能發出菩提心，那個時候我們都成為僧人了，都是三寶之一，可以說是一切眾生的怙主、皈依處了。

When we arouse bodhichitta, then we will all become Sangha, one of the Three Jewels, and we can be said to be glorious protectors and refuge for all sentient beings.

你不敢相信自己是佛，這就是你的業障，別的沒有業障。

You dare not believe yourself being the Buddha, which is your own karma, no other karma.

如果你有一顆恭敬心、虔誠心，實物供養和意幻供養沒有任何區別。

If you are respectful and sincere, there will be no difference in the ways of offering, whether with material objects or in mind.

實際上任何人都有佛性，如果你真正認識到了，你就解脫了。

As a matter of fact, everyone has the Buddha-nature. If you really realize it, you will be liberated.

只有善的起心動念，才能成為得到各種資糧和福報的因。有了足夠的福德資糧，才能成就世間和出世間的一切。

Only motivations out of kindness can become the causes of various prerequisites and merits. Only with enough merits and virtues, can one obtain mundane or transmundane achievements successfully.

我們不是要逃避，而是要面對。我們敢面對敢承担的時候，才沒有畏懼，沒有恐怖。沒有畏懼感、恐怖感，沒有患得患失，才沒有煩惱和痛苦。

We should not escape but face. When we are brave enough to confront and take responsibilities, we will not suffer from fears or terrors. Without the sense of terror, and without the worries of gains and loss, we will break away from afflictions and pains.

人都有佛性，都能成佛是指：每個人都可以學功德，修福報，而且可以學到圓滿，修到圓滿。

Everyone has Buddha-nature and can become the Buddha, which means that everyone can learn merits, practice blessings, and what's more, everyone can attain perfection through learning and practicing.

佛法跟一般的學問不一樣，佛法是從恭敬心和信心中得來的，有恭敬心和信心才能成就。

Dharma, which can be attained from respect and faith, is different from general learning. Only with respect and faith can one succeed.

恭敬心和信心是從修行，從消業積福中來的。業障越小，福報越大，對上師三寶的信心越大。

Respect and faith come from practicing, eliminating bad karma and accumulating merits. The less one's karma is, the more one's merits are, and the more faith one has in the Guru and the Three Jewels.

你所修的法是正法還是邪法，就看你相續中的煩惱和習氣有沒有減少——如果有減少，你所修的法就是正法。

Whether you are practicing true Dharma or false Dharma depends on whether the annoyances and bad habits in your continuity have decreased-if they have decreased, then what you are practicing is true Dharma.

執着世間、執着世間法是執着；執着佛、執着佛法也是執着。只要是執着，就一定會有煩惱。

There is no difference between the attachment to the world or the worldly matters and the attachment to Buddha or Dharma-both of the two are attachments. As long as there exist attachments, annoyance will come along together.

執着是煩惱的根，煩惱是痛苦的根。有煩惱就會造業，造業了就會感受痛苦。

Attachment is the root of annoyance, and in turn, annoyance is the root of pains. With annoyance, one tends to create karma, and with karma, one will suffer from pains.

在證悟空性以前，我們還沒有找到自己的心，都在愚癡的狀態中，所做的一切都是惡，都是輪迴的因。

Before the realization of emptiness, we haven't found our heart, lying in a state of ignorance, so what we do are all vicious deeds, which are the causes of samsara.

觀察、評論他人的過失本身就是一種過失。

To observe and comment on others' faults is a fault itself.

我們要養成一種良好的品質，善於去觀察、發現、欣賞生活與他人美好善良的一面，然後將之變為一種習慣。這樣我們在思想與行為上才能逐漸變得高尚與純粹，才能真正與佛法相應。

We need to form a good quality, that is to become good at observing, finding and appreciating the good aspects of life and other people, and then turn it into a habit. Only in this way can we become noble and pure, both in mind and in action, and become really consistent with Dharma.

什麼時候能夠隨緣，什麼時候才能順利。當你無所求時，才會無所不有。

When you are ready to follow causes and conditions, everything will turn out well. When you pursue nothing, you will get everything.

福報不是求來的，是修來的；煩惱不是別人給的，是自己找的。

One gets merits not by pursuing, but by practicing; annoyance comes not from others, but from self.

寂靜處不在山上，也不在廟裡，只要有一顆清淨心，到處都有寂靜處，到處都是淨土。

The Aranya is neither in the mountain nor in the temple. As long as you have a pure mind, everywhere is the Aranya, everywhere is pure land.

任何時候都要靠他力和自力——上師三寶的力量和自己的力量，結合在一起才有感應，才有成就。

Achievements rely on both self-power and others power all times-only when the power from the Guru and the Three Jewels and the power from self combine together can there be interaction and achievements.

本來具有的清淨平等的自性，就是佛性。每一個眾生本來都具足跟阿彌陀佛、釋迦牟尼佛一樣，一點也不差的佛性。

The innate pure and equal nature is Buddha-nature. Each being from the beginning fully possesses the Buddha-nature which is exactly as good as what Buddha Amitabha or Buddha Sakyamuni has.

我們總是喜歡攀緣，不肯隨緣。原因就是怕不順利。但攀緣是不會順利的，即使順利了也是暫時的，不是永久的。

We are used to clinging about rather than following the cause and condition. The reason is the fear of unsmoothness. However, clinging about doesn't bring smoothness, even it does, the smoothness so brought will just be temporary rather than permanent.

真正隨緣了，才能順利；真正放下了，才能得到。

Truly follow cause and condition, then may smoothness come; truly let go, then may you achieve.

修行人應該是很正常、很恆順的人，無論什麼時候都不惱害他人，也不白生煩惱，這才是圓滿。

Practitioners shall be very normal and agreeable people, never annoying others or self at any time, and this is the perfection only.

現在我們學佛、修行了，有時候惱害眾生，有時候自尋煩惱，這都不如法。學佛、修行太執着了，也是一種障礙。

Now we are learning and practicing Dharma, however, sometimes we still annoy other beings or afflict ourselves, and all of these are not correct. Too obsessed in learning and practicing is also an obstacle.

諸佛菩薩所有的願行都包含在普賢菩薩十大願望裡，這裡有恆順眾生。你能恆順眾生，就是學佛、修行。

All practices and aspirations of Buddhas and Bodhisattvas are included in the Ten Great Aspirations of Bodhisattva Samantabhadra, where being agreeable to all beings is included. If you can be agreeable to all beings, then you are learning and practicing.

在任何對境面前都沒有分別，就是平等心；在任何情況下都不起煩惱，就是清淨心。你能發平等心、清淨心，無論做什麼事都是善事。

It is the mind of equality if you have no discrimination when confronting any objects; it is the mind of purity if you can keep from arousing afflictions under any circumstances. If you have the mind of equality and purity, whatever you do will be virtuous.

你的相續中是否有真正的出離心,是否有無偽的慈悲心和菩提心。如果有了,加行才算修成了,你才能成為法器,才可以修正行。

Do you have true renunciation, genuine compassion and bodhichitta in your continuity? Only you do, can it be said that you have successfully completed the preliminary practices, and can you become the suitable recipient for Dharma and start the main practice.

心放平了，一切都會風平浪靜；心放正了，一切都會一帆風順；心放下了，永恆的安樂與幸福也就隨之而來了。

*W*hen you feel the inner peace, everything around you will be tranquil; when you feel upright in mind, everything will go well; when you let go of everything, the long-lasting peace and happiness will follow.

365天的加持

人的命運完全掌握在自己手上，關鍵是怎麼調伏這顆心。三藏十二部、八萬四千法門，都是調伏心的方法。如果心沒有安住，還是沒有真正的修行。

We have our fate in our hands but the problem is how to control our mind. The Tripitaka, the twelve divisions and the eighty-four thousand Dharma gates are all ways to balance our minds. If we don't have peace in mind, we are not practicing the Dharma.

 *365 Days Of Blessings*

怎樣才能生起信心？只有消業、積福，才能生起具足的信心。業障小了，福報大了，信心自然就具足了。

How to build up confidence? Only by eliminating the bad karma and accumulating good merits, can we have adequate confidence, because with the evil things getting less and less and the good fortune becoming more and more, we can naturally have sufficient confidence.

有平穩的心、知足的心,就是你最大的福報。

The biggest fortune for you is to have a peaceful and contented mind

人要有智慧。事情本身沒有好和壞，好壞是我們自己的分別、執着。

Individuals should have wisdom. All the things themselves are not good or bad; it is us who separate them into good and bad with our minds.

真正有修行了，世間上的成就才不會成為你痛苦和壓力的來源。

Only when you practice the Dharma whole-heartedly, can all the worldly accomplishments never be your causes of pain and stress.

在所有的活法當中，我們選擇了學佛修行，這不是一般人能做到的。

Among all the ways to live our life, we choose to practice Dharma, which is not an easy choice or task for ordinary people.

無始劫以來，我們都患有貪嗔癡慢疑五毒病，這不是一般的病。患上這些病，我們就會斷掉解脫的慧命，會感受輪迴的痛苦。

Since the beginningless kalpa, we have the five kinds of disease: greed, anger, ignorance, arrogance and doubt, and these diseases are not easy to recover from. When we get these diseases, we are going to lose our wisdom-life for relief and suffer from the samsara.

 *365 Days Of Blessings*

一切痛苦都是由貪嗔癡等煩惱造成的，我們要了解這些痛苦，並且擺脫它們。

All the pains are caused by greed, anger and ignorance, so we need to know these pains and get rid of them.

六月二十四日　　　　　　*24th, June*

不用問別人自己能否修成，自己最清楚自己，只要有希求正法的心，就能修成。這是最標準的答案。

You don't need to ask others whether you can complete the practice because it should be you who know yourself best. If you have an eager mind for the true Dharma, then you can make it. And this is the only answer.

365 Days Of Blessings

煩惱是執着來的，痛苦也是執着來的。你覺得不好，想不通，想不開，就是愚癡，因為不會換角度。

All the bothers come from obsession and so do all the pains. If you feel bad and cannot think through, then you are in the ignorance, because you are not able to think from another perspective.

一切人、一切事物都是兩面的。好的地方是用佛心看的，不好的地方是用凡夫心看的。佛只看好的地方，都觀為清淨圓滿；凡夫只看不好的地方，所以在一切境界中都會被影響、被傷害。

Everyone and everything has two sides, good and bad. Those with Buddha mind can always see the good side while those with human-mind can only see the bad side. Buddha only sees purity and completeness, while human only sees bad things so they can be easily affected and hurt.

 *365 Days Of Blessings*

懂得了因果，也就掌握了改變命運的方法。

Understanding causes and effects is mastering the key to changing your fate.

讀經固然好，讀心更重要。

Reading Sutra is good while understanding the mind is more important.

不相信輪迴就是不相信佛法，沒有取捨因果就是沒有修持佛法。真正相信輪迴才可能不再執着輪迴，真正相信因果才可能不再造惡業。

If you do not believe in samsara then you do not trust Dharma; if you do not practice causes and effects then you are not practicing Dharma. Only when you truly believe the existence of samsara, can you give up obsession with samsara; only when you truly believe in causes and effects, can you stop doing evil things.

365天的加持

學佛就是了緣、了債、了生死。

*S*tudying Dharma is to end the destiny, to pay the debt and to end the life and death.

如果你真正明白了人身難得，壽命無常，因果不虛，輪迴痛苦，真正清楚了解脫的利益，就會認識到修行的重要。

When you really understand the difficulty of getting a human body, the impermanence of life, the existence of causes and effects, the pain of samsara, and the benefits of getting liberation, then you can fully realize the importance of practicing Dharma.

365天的加持

沒有恆常不變的東西！別當真，都是假相，都在演戲。

There is no permanent thing. Don't take it to be real, because everything is fake and acting.

在修行的過程中一定要多發心、發願，跟這些眾生結善緣，不能結惡緣。我們跟眾生結的善緣越多，修行就越順利；我們跟眾生結的惡緣越多，修行上的障礙就越多。

When practicing the Dharma, we need to arouse aspirations and make vows, and when we are making connections with the beings we should only make good connections instead of bad ones. When we have more and more good connections with the beings, we can practice the Dharma more smoothly and vise versa.

365天的加持

不要總是按照自己的想法要求別人，一定要按照別人的想法要求自己。

Don't always attempt to ask others do things with your thoughts, do ask yourself to do with others' thoughts.

不為他人着想，永遠得不到想要的東西。

When careless of the other people's needs, then never could you get what you want.

不管是什麼緣，既然結了就要了，這叫隨緣。

No matter what kind of connection you have made, once it is made, you have to fulfill it; this is called following the causes and conditions.

你既然已經發心、發願了，就要去做啊！否則就是欺騙上師三寶，欺騙父母眾生，這是罪過呀！

If you have already made aspirational wishes, then you should try the best to accomplish it! Otherwise, you are lying to the Guru and the Three Jewels, lying to the sentient beings, this is sin!

佛法應該是自在的，你沒有自由自在，就沒有佛法。

While practicing Buddhism, one should feel free and happy. Without this feeling, then there is no Buddhism.

命運可以改變，可以轉。隨什麼轉？隨着你的心轉。這個心就是善心和惡心、善業和惡業。

*F*ate can be changed, can be altered. Altered with what? With your heart. This heart is so called good heart and evil heart, good karma and bad karma.

出離心就是對輪迴沒有絲毫的貪戀，對世間法沒有絲毫的貪圖。我們不是要脫離輪迴，而是要脫離輪迴的苦。學佛修行就是脫離這些痛苦的方法。

Renunciation means no attachment to samsara, no attachment to the worldly things. We are not trying to get rid of samsara, but the pain of the samsara. Practicing Buddhism is the path of keeping the pain away.

 *365 Days Of Blessings*

不自由的轉叫輪迴。我們不能這樣轉，我們要自由的轉，這叫弘揚佛法、救度眾生。

*T*ransmigration without freedom is samsara. We should not transmigrate like this, we should transmigrate freely, and this is called spreading Buddhism and liberating the sentient beings.

我們每做一件事的時候，都去給別人表法，使別人感化，讓別人也學習佛法，修持佛法，這叫救度眾生。

Everything we do is to show the Dharma to the others, warm the others, let the others study Buddhism, practice Buddhism as well, this is called liberating the sentient beings.

365 Days Of Blessings

我們一定要學會面對現實。真會面對了，就不會煩惱、痛苦了。

We must learn to face the reality. When you really know how to face it, then there will be no more suffering, no more pain.

沒有超越因果的時候，就不能超越輪迴，還要在輪迴裡感受痛苦；超越了因果，才能超越輪迴。之前，不管是念佛還是修法，只能得到人天的福報，得到暫時的利益，根本不能解脫。

When you are unable to surpass the cause and effect, then you cannot transcend the samsara, will still live in pain of the samsara; when you surpass the cause and effect, you may transcend the samsara. Before that, whether you are reciting mantra or practicing Dharma, you can only obtain the merits of Human and God realms, obtain the temporary benefit, but not the liberation.

 *365 Days Of Blessings*

有分別的念是雜念，有分別的修是雜修。沒有分別的念，沒有分別的修，這是真正的專修、專念。

The discriminative thoughts is distracting thoughts, the discriminative practice is distracting practice. Only without the discriminative thoughts and practice, this is the true practice and study.

有的人逃避心特別強，一講輪迴過患，講地獄、餓鬼、傍生的痛苦，就不願意聽，這都是逃避心，都是執着。

Some people have strong tendency to run away, dislike to talk about the defects of samsara, the suffering of hell, preta and animal realms. This is the runaway mind, which is attachment.

 *365 Days Of Blessings*

把輪迴看透了，才不會害怕。我們現在總是害怕，總想逃避，不敢面對。這是因為我們沒有弄明白輪迴到底是怎麼回事。如果弄明白了，是不會這樣害怕的，內心會得到一種快樂與安定。

If you truly understand the samsara, then there will be no fear. We are always afraid, want to escape, afraid to face, this is because we don't understand the samsara, if you understand, you won't be so afraid, you will have the happiness and peace in your heart.

七月十八日　　18th, July

不要總是牽掛，放不下，各有各的因緣，各有各的福報，盡到你的責任和義務就行了。

Do not always hold on to your thought, hard to let go, everything has its own cause and condition, everyone has his own merits, do your best to fulfill your responsibility, that is all!

365 Days Of Blessings

不要回憶過去，不要迎接未來，也不要執着現在。把心自然安住下來，不控制它，不跟隨它，不阻攔它，也不拒絕它。讓它來去自由，放鬆，放下，把它放到本覺當中，真正做到了，就成佛了。

Do not recall the past, do not receive the future, do not attach to present. Give your heart a place to stay, no control, no follow, no refuse. Let go freely, relax, let go, put it in the primordial state, if you truly can do it, then you have obtained the Buddhahood.

成佛是在做人的基礎上，先做人，再做佛。連人都沒有做好，怎麼能做佛呢？

To obtain the Buddhahood is based on what kind of a human being you are, be the good person first, then the Buddha. If you are not a good person, no way can you become a Buddha.

每個眾生都和自己
一樣，你對自己
怎樣，也一定要對眾
生怎樣。

Every sentient being is like yourself, how you treat yourself, you should treat the sentient beings just the same.

捨棄了眾生就等於捨棄了菩提心，捨棄了眾生就等於捨棄了佛法。

Giving up sentient beings is giving up bodhichitta, giving up sentient beings is giving up Buddhism.

對自己沒有信心就是對佛法沒有信心！如果對佛法有信心，肯定對自己也有信心。

*N*ot believing in yourself is not believing in the Dharma! If you believe in Buddhism, you must believe in yourself.

佛讓我們放下，我們為什麼放不下？總是執着、牽掛，着急、上火？沒有別的原因，就是害怕。已得到的，怕失去；未得到的，怕得不到，患得患失！

Buddha told us to let go, why can't we? Why are we always attached, worried or upset? No other reasons but fear. Afraid to lose what you have; afraid not to get what you still do not have, afraid of gain and loss.

沒有智慧的人，沒有方便，所以有違緣障礙；有智慧的人，有方便，所以沒有違緣障礙。有違緣障礙，就有煩惱痛苦。

The people lacking wisdom have no expedients, so they run into obstacles; the people with wisdom have the expedients, so they have no obstacles. The obstacles create sufferings.

365天的加持

覺得這個好，就去追求；覺得那個不好，就想逃避。總在患得患失的牢獄中，這樣你永遠解脫不了。不會有輕鬆自在，也不會有快樂幸福。

Pursue the good because feeling it is good; escape the bad because feeling it is bad. Deeply involved in the worry of gain and loss, you can never get liberation, nor can you have ease and joy.

 *365 Days Of Blessings*

了緣就是一定要盡到自己的責任和義務。否則你沒有修行，不能解脫，不能成佛。

Fulfilling karma is doing your best to take responsibility and pay your duty. Otherwise, you are not practicing Dharma, nor can you get liberation and attain Buddhahood.

信念是值得你付出生命的。

Belief is worth paying your life.

金剛兄弟之間一定要團結和睦。我們有團結，有和睦，才有共同的力量。我們的力量就是加持，力量在一起，加持就在一起。

Harmony and Unity are very important value between Vajra Brothers. Strength is from the unity and harmony, our strength is the blessing. Strength is unified, the blessing is unified.

了脫生死的意思是了脫生死的苦。佛也生，也死，但是不受生死的苦；凡夫執着，沒有智慧，要受生死的苦。

The meaning of liberation from the birth and death is to liberate from the pain of birth and death. The Buddha also experiences the birth and death, but he has no pain; the ordinary people are attached to things for having little wisdom, so they have to experience the pain of samsara.

解脱成就以後也有因果，但是不受因果。我們還沒有解脫，沒有成就，還要受因果。我們只能轉變因果，別的沒有辦法。

After the liberation and enlightenment, one will still follow the law of cause and effect, but will not be affected. We are not liberated or accomplished, so we have to take the effect. We can only change the cause and effect, no other methods.

365天的加持

千萬不能把相續和佛法分開，不能把生活和修行分開，分開是過錯，這樣你永遠都不會解脫。

Never separate your continuity from Dharma, never separate your life from practice. It is wrong to seperate them and never will you obtain liberation.

你所擁有的財產、機會、權利等，都是自己生生世世修來的福報，浪費這些就是浪費自己的福報，這個道理一定要清楚！

The wealth, opportunity and the power you have obtained are all the merits you have accumulated in all the past lives, wasting them means wasting your merits, so do be clear about it.

佛力加持不可思議。找到了解脫的方向，繼續堅持修，認真修，老老實實修，不能退轉。時時刻刻祈禱上師三寶加持，就不會有違緣和障礙。

Buddha's blessing is unimaginable. As you have found the path to liberation, practice continually, diligently and truly, never draw back. Pray to the Guru and the Three Jewels for blessings all the time, you will have no ill fate and obstacles.

 *365 Days Of Blessings*

念佛念心，修行修心。時時刻刻觀察自己的心，時時刻刻調整自己的心態。

Reciting Buddha's name is reading your mind, while practicing Buddhism is practicing your mind. Observe your mind every moment, and adjust your attitude all the time.

把修行放在第一位，沒有什麼事比修行更重要，除非你不想解脫。

Put dharma practice the first, nothing is more important than practice, unless you don't want liberation.

佛即是心，心即是佛。有的人不念心念相，不觀心觀相。追求形式，執着表相；不信真佛，不拜真佛，不供真佛。這樣永遠也成不了佛。

Buddha means heart, heart means Buddha. Some people care about not the heart but the image, and do not look into the heart but into the appearance, only minding the form, attaching to appearance; having no trust in true Buddha, not paying homage and making offering to true Buddha. In this manner, one can never obtain the Buddhahood.

什麼是竅訣？能讓你證悟空性實義、證悟本性，把心安住在本覺當中的這個方法，叫竅訣。

What is pith-instruction? It is the way to help you to reach the enlightenment, understand the true nature, keep the heart in the primordial state, this is called pith instruction.

如果你真正得到灌頂了，你的相續中肯定有無比的信心、強烈的出離心、無偽的慈悲心和菩提心。如果沒有，你還是沒有得到灌頂，你還不是灌頂的法器。

If you have really got the empowerment, then your continuity must have incomparable faith, strong renunciation, truthful compassion and bodhichitta. If not, then you have not yet received the empowerment, you are not yet the recipient for the empowerment.

365天的加持

每一個起心動念都是關鍵的時刻。時時刻刻觀察自己的心相續，把每個起心動念都轉換到善知善念、正知正見上，這就是斷惡行善。

Every thought passed in your mind is the moment of importance. Observe the mind continuity at each moment, alter all your thoughts to the virtue and right view, this is stopping all evils and doing all good deeds.

不執着對境，一切隨緣，你才能脫離痛苦，這是我們學佛的目的。

Don't be attached to an object, let it be, then you are able to be free from suffering, this is the purpose of studying Buddhism.

菩提心發出來了，修哪種法都能達到圓滿，念多少佛都是念一尊佛，所有的佛與自己的本尊都是一體的。

As the bodhichitta is generated, all the Dharma practice leads to completeness, all Buddhas' names recited are the recitation of the same Buddha, all Buddhas and the Yidam of self are the same unity.

如果你有希求正法的心，在家、出家都能學會，都能修成。如果沒有希求正法的心，在家、出家都一樣是虛度光陰，荒廢人身。

If you have the heart wishing for Dharma, being a lay practitioner or being a monk makes no difference, your practice will complete. If you don't pursue the true Dharma, then no matter where you practice, both the time and human life are wasted.

什麼是魔？方便地說，讓你心亂、煩惱、痛苦的都是魔。如果你的心動了，它擾亂了你心的清淨，它就變成魔了；如果你的心不動，心清淨了，一切都是佛，哪裡有魔呢？

What is Mara? In brief, anything that makes you disturbed, afflictive or painful is Mara. If your mind is unstable, and its purity is disturbed, then the mind turns into Mara; if your mind is clear, is pure, then everything is Buddha, no Mara can be found anywhere.

不拒絕，也不追求，這都是緣起，緣起的本性就是佛性。

No refusal, no pursuit, all these are dependent origination, the nature of which is the true nature of Buddhism.

看一個人修行如何，不是看表相，而是看他對有情眾生是否有真實無偽的慈悲心、菩提心，對上師三寶是否有堅定不移的信心，貪嗔癡等煩惱、習氣是否在減少。

How to tell a person's practice is not on his superficial appearance, but on whether the person is able to generate the true compassion and bodhichitta, whether he has the truthful and irremovable faith to the Guru and the Three Jewels, whether his desire, hatred and ignorance and bad habit are diminishing.

 *365 Days Of Blessings*

什麼時候真的看破了，從心裡放下了，才不受因果。否則，受因果就有煩惱，有煩惱就有痛苦。

Whenever you really are able to see through and let go from the bottom of your heart, you are out of cause and effect. Otherwise, when you are still affected by cause and effect, then you still have sufferings and pains.

不放棄任何人，不放棄任何事，才是圓滿。

Do not give up anyone; do not give up anything, this is accomplishment

順境和逆境是凡夫分別出來的。如果你執着了，心動了，這就是逆境；如果你放下了，心不動，一切都是順境。

Favourable and unfavourable conditions are the thoughts of human mind. If you are attached, your mind is not stable, then this is the unfavourable condition; if you are detached, your mind is clear, everything is favourable condition.

大富大貴不難，平平安安難；吃喝玩樂不難，自由自在難！

It is not difficult to accumulate great wealth, but hard to be in peace; it is easy to have a life of pleasure, but difficult to get freedom.

放下不是放棄，輕鬆不是懈怠，自在不是放逸，隨緣不是隨便，不執着不是不認真。

Let-go is not give-up, leisure is not being lazy, enjoying is not indulgence, let-it-be is not careless, and detaching is not paying less attention.

八月二十一日　　*21st, August*

有病不怕，機會來了。有病是消業、還債的機會，修慈悲心、菩提心的機會。有病時發大願，發大心，觀想和自己同樣病苦的眾生的痛苦由自己一人承担，病很快就能好。任何病都能好。

Do not worry about being sick, it is good opportunity. Sickness is the chance for you to purify, pay back the debt, the chance to cultivate the compassion and bodhichitta. Generate the great aspiration and good will when you are sick, visualize the sufferings of all sick beings is taken by you alone, then you will recover soon, every sickness will be gone.

365 Days Of Blessings

你真正從內心裡發出了慈悲心、菩提心，冤親債主才不會再找你。他知道你在修行，將來能度化他，他不會找你麻煩，反而會喜歡你，保護你，幫助你，成為你的護法。這是改變命運的方法。

The true compassion and bodhichitta generated from your heart will ease the hatred from your karmic creditor. He knows you are practicing the Dharma and you will have the ability to liberate him in the future, he won't make trouble for you, instead he will like you, protect you, help you, and become your Dharma protector. This is the way to change your fate.

修慈悲心是你一定要把眾生當作自己的父母，修菩提心是你一定要把眾生當作佛。

To practice compassion, you need to consider all sentient beings are your parents; to practice bodhichitta, you need to take all beings as Buddhas.

學佛修行就是用智慧給自己創造美好的生活。

Study and practice Buddhism is to create a beautiful life for self with wisdom.

出離心是解脫的方法，菩提心是快樂的方法。

Renunciation is the path to liberation; bodhichitta is the path to happiness.

一切時、一切處、一切境界中，念念不忘上師三寶，念念不忘父母眾生，念念不忘如法修行。

In all times, all places, all states of mind, never forget the Guru and the Three Jewels, never forget the parental beings, and never forget to practice Dharma.

365天的加持

被他人傷害了，應該懺悔自己。

If you are hurt by others, you should confess yourself.

沒有煩惱才是解脫，沒有習氣才是成佛。

Liberation means having no afflictive emotions, Buddhahood means having no bad habits.

我們現在所受到的傷害全部來自於對輪迴、對世間瑣事的貪愛與牽掛。

All the hurts we are experiencing come from the desire and attachment to the worldly things and samsara.

修行人永遠不會寂寞，因為十方三世一切諸佛菩薩時刻都在關注着你，圍繞着你。

Practitioners can never feel lonely, because all Buddha from the ten directions and three times are with you and surround you.

發大心，發大願；發清淨的心，發清淨的願。什麼也比不過清淨心、清淨願的力量！在這個上下功夫！

Generate great mind, make great wishes; generate pure mind, make pure wishes. Nothing could be stronger than generating pure mind! Practice on this diligently.

在這個世界上沒有無緣無故的愛與恨，都是因緣果報。

In this world there is no love or hate without reason, all is karmic retribution.

有的人從少到老，一直追求想要的東西，經歷了很多坎坷和磨難，付出了無數的代價，卻什麼也沒有得到，這就是窩囊！

Some people have been chasing what they want from young until old, experienced lots of hardships and sufferings, paid numerous prices, however, they finally end up with getting nothing, this is incapable.

 365 Days Of Blessings

法喜充滿地念，才叫信心。

Only when you chant with your mind filled with Dharma joy can it be called faith.

看到別人的缺點與毛病，要好好地反思自己，這是自己的缺點、毛病，是自己的業障，是自己的福報、智慧不夠。

While we are observing other people's weakness and defects, we should reflect ourselves carefully and realize that these are our own weakness and defects, and our own karmic obscurations, it is because of the inadequacy of our own wisdom and blessings.

 *365 Days Of Blessings*

認識到我們的所見所聞，包括此生，都是假相，都是虛幻，才能真正認識到諸法的真相。

Not until we have realized what we saw and heard, as well as this life are all illusional and unreal can we thoroughly wake up to the truth of Dharma.

是要眼前的利益，還是要永久的利益？是要眼前的快樂，還是要永恆的快樂？想得到永恆的，就要放下眼前的。

Do you want temporary interest or permanent interest? Do you want temporary happiness or permanent happiness? If you want the permanent one, you have to give up the temporary one.

只有開發內心的慈
悲和智慧，才能
達到生死自在。

Only those who develop their inner mercy and wisdom can be free from life and death.

想過關，就要不斷地去面對、去經歷。

If you want to get past, you have to face and undergo it constantly.

什麼叫禪定？心專注於一個境當中而不散亂。

*W*hat is meditation?
Devote your mind
to a certain realm and keep
it from scattering.

你修行的層次越高，自身的變化越大，對別人的影響也越大。

The higher practice level you reach, the greater transformation you get, the bigger your influence on others will be.

觀照自己的心，就是要知道自己在想些什麼，做些什麼，隨時將惡的念頭轉換為善的念頭。

Watching your mind is to be aware of what you are thinking, what you are doing, and transform evil thoughts into virtuous ones in no time.

當我們的心邪惡的
時候，我們就是
「魔」；當我們的心
良善的時候，我們就
是「佛」。

*W*hile our mind
is with vicious
thoughts, we are "devils";
while our mind is with
virtuous ones, we are
"Buddhas".

也許剛開始的時候，我們總是「魔」，怎麼也不是「佛」，但是只要我們不放棄自己，總有一天會成「佛」的，成為真正的「佛」。

Maybe, at the very beginning, we are "devils" all the time; whatever we do, we aren't "Buddhas". But, as long as we never give up, one day, we will become "Buddhas", true "Buddhas".

365天的加持

我們都有缺點、煩惱、習氣，這些都需要通過修行才能去掉。

All of us are born with shortcomings, negative emotions and habitual tendencies, which need to be dispelled only through Dharma practice.

 *365 Days Of Blessings*

只看自己的缺點、毛病，不看自己的優點、功德。自己那點微不足道的功德和上師三寶的功德比起來算什麼呢？

We should look on our shortcomings and faults only, but not our virtues and merits. How insignificant our merits are when compared with those of our Guru and the Three Jewels?

365天的加持

有些東西你越要，它離你越遠；你越不要，它離你越近；你真要的時候都不來，你真不要的時候什麼都來。

There are some things, the more you pursue, the farther they go; the less you pursue, the closer they come; they never come when you are really pursuing, but come when you are really not pursuing.

什麼叫利根者？對上師，對佛法，對自己有信心——「我會」、「我能」、「我肯定會」、「我肯定能」，這叫利根者。

Who is the one with sharp faculties? Being faithful to the Guru, the Dharma and self, believing "I will", "I can", "I surely will", "I surely can", this kind of person is called the one with sharp faculties.

我們一定要在對境中修行，想逃避現實是不可能的，關鍵是怎麼面對。

We must practice Dharma when facing objects, since hoping to escape from reality is impossible. The key is how to face it.

365 Days Of Blessings

一切隨緣，操心沒有用，不能解決問題。任何事情都不能通過操心解決。

Let it be. Worry is useless, and it doesn't work. Nothing can be solved through worry.

你周圍人的變化，就是你修行的進步。

The transformation of the people around you is the progress you have got.

如果你了解上師三寶的功德，並且喜歡這些功德，也下決心想得到這些功德，那個時候你才能得到加持，才能得到這些功德。

If you know about and like the merits and virtues of your Guru and the Three Jewels, and also make up your mind to gain them, only then can you receive the blessing and gain these merits and virtues.

生命是暫時的，慧命是永恆的，要用生命來保護慧命，不能用慧命來保護生命。

Life is impermanent, while wisdom life is permanent. We should use life to protect wisdom life but not the reverse.

即便其它什麼法都不修，只修上師瑜伽，也能獲得成就。

Even if you never practice all other Dharma teachings except for Guru Yoga, you can also get realization.

真正的佛法是能對治煩惱、習氣的。如果你的煩惱少了，習氣輕了，雖然還沒有徹底斷除，但說明你已經有修行了，得到正法了。堅持下去，有一天肯定會戰勝這些煩惱、習氣，這才是真正的解脫、圓滿。

The real Dharma can cure negative emotions and habitual tendencies. If your negative emotions become fewer, and your habitual tendencies become lighter, though they are not completely eradicated, it shows you have made some progress and got benefited from the real Dharma. Keep going, and one day you will surely overcome these negative emotions and habitual tendencies, this is the real liberation and completeness.

 *365 Days Of Blessings*

我們不能對輪迴有貪圖和執着。如果有了，就脫離不了輪迴，遠離不了痛苦。

We should not covet or cling to samsara. If we fail, we can neither get out of samsara nor keep far away from suffering.

真正能夠放下的時候，你的智慧就圓滿了。那個時候，人都是好人，都是佛；處都是好處，都是淨土；事都是好事，都是助緣。

When you can really let things go, your wisdom is completed. At that time, everybody is a nice person, the Buddha; everywhere is a perfect place, the Pure Land; everything is a good thing, the aiding condition.

 *365 Days Of Blessings*

統統地把「我」忘掉，不要總帶着「我」，摻雜「我」。不要這個「我」了，為眾生活着吧！

Wholly forget "self", never taking or mingling with "self" all the time. Don't covet this "self", live for all beings.

聖者和凡夫的區別在於思想。凡夫只看眼前利益，而聖者看長遠利益。

The distinction between saints and ordinary persons is thoughts. An ordinary person pursues short-term interests, while a saint chases long-term ones.

犯錯誤不是問題，人不可能不犯錯誤。如果明明知道自己犯錯了還不改正，犯戒了還不懺悔，這才是最大的問題，這樣永遠解脫不了。

Making mistakes isn't a problem, because it's impossible for human beings to keep doing right. If you clearly know you've already done wrong but still keep on it, or you've broken the precepts but still do not confess them, this is the biggest problem. In this way, you won't get liberated forever.

365天的加持

只有自己的心障礙
自己，別的沒有
什麼障礙。不相信不
可思議，就見不到宇
宙人生的真相。

There is not any other obstacle except your own mind. Not believing in inconceivable things, then you cannot see the truth of cosmos and life.

在輪迴裡，感覺不到苦，是不可能的。

In samsara, it's impossible to fail to feel the misery.

世間的聰明不等於智慧，世間的財富不等於福報。財福不是真正的福，法福才是真正的福。

Worldly cleverness isn't equal to wisdom, and worldly treasure isn't equal to merits. The fortune of wealth isn't the real fortune while the fortune of Dharma is.

如果你有感恩心，有慈悲心，有想學法修行的決心，就沒有什麼做不到的！

If you have a grateful heart, a compassionate heart, a determination of practicing Dharma, there is nothing you cannot achieve.

慈悲心、菩提心發出來了，無論做什麼，都是為眾生，都有功德；無論說什麼，都是咒語，都是智慧。

Once your compassion and bodhichitta are aroused, whatever you do, you are doing for all beings, which have merits and virtues; whatever you say, you are chanting mantra, which is wisdom indeed.

從內心裡，心甘情願，特別迫切地受戒，這是一種享受。如果受戒的時候，覺得苦，覺得有壓力，說明你的發心還不到位。

Being eager to take the precepts from deep in your heart with willingness, this is a kind of enjoyment. If you feel bitter or pressured while you are receiving precepts, which shows your aspiration hasn't been fully aroused.

我們為什麼得不到加持？因為對上師三寶不是深信不疑、一心一意，而是半信半疑、三心二意，關鍵的時候都不相信。難就難在這裡。

Why can't we receive blessings? It is because we don't believe in our Guru and the Three Jewels firmly and wholeheartedly, but dubiously and half-heartedly, especially at crucial moments. This is the very difficulty.

有正知正見才能降伏邪知邪見。正知正見是覺，不是迷。不知道阿彌陀佛是怎麼回事，還念「阿彌陀佛」，這就是迷。迷本身是一種邪見，以邪知邪見來降伏邪知邪見，哪有這樣的修法啊？

Only the clear awareness and the right views can vanquish evil understanding and wrong views. The clear awareness and the right views are enlightenment rather than delusion. Chanting "Amitabha" without learning about what it means, this is delusion. Delusion itself is a kind of wrong view. Using wrong views to subdue wrong views, how can there be such practice?

我們為了眾生要成佛，但是也要有因緣，沒有因緣，無緣無故的不能成佛。成佛的因緣是行菩薩道。我們能做到六度等菩薩的學處，才能成佛。

Vowing to become a Buddha for all beings, but there should be some certain conditions, without which no one can become a Buddha. The condition of attaining Buddhahood is to practice the Bodhisattva teachings. Only when we can perform the six transcendent perfections and other bodhichitta trainings, can we become Buddha.

 *365 Days Of Blessings*

我們在修行的過程中，有些時候，有些地方，沒有做到很正常。如果不知道自己沒有做到，既不注意，也不改正，這才是問題，這是造業！

During our practice, it is quite normal to fail at some times or in some aspects. But if we don't know about it, neither paying attention, nor correcting, this is the real problem. It is creating karma.

你認為出現違緣、障礙了，然後害怕了，就錯了！這是沒有智慧！這都是最好的機會。如果把握住了，這些就能讓你成就；如果把握不住，這些就會讓你煩惱。

You think there are obstacles and barriers, and you feel afraid. Actually, you are wrong. This is because of your lack of wisdom. These are the best chances for your practice. If you can get hold of them successfully, they will help you gain achievement; if not, they will make you suffer.

 *365 Days Of Blessings*

不要評價任何人，我們沒有這個資格。我們還是凡夫，不知道別人的發心、動機與成就。這樣會造業的。

*D*o not evaluate anyone else, since we don't have this qualification. We are still ordinary persons, unaware of others' aspirations, motivations and accomplishments. Doing so will lead us to create karma.

自己是自己最大的敵人！身體上所有疾病的來源都是自己的心。如果內心不清淨、不安寧的話，無論怎樣講衛生、講營養，身體依然會受到傷害。

We ourselves are our greatest enemies! The source of all the physical diseases is our mind. If our mind is not pure, not in peace, however we pay attention to hygiene or nutrition, our bodies will still get hurt.

十月十三日　　13th, October

不要混日子，樣樣事都好好做，明明白白地做，用心做，這就是修行！

Don't laze away. Do everything seriously, clearly, whole-heartedly, this is practice.

現在很多人小事不去做，大事做不了，結果什麼也沒有做成。不管是小事還是大事，家裡事還是家外事，個人事還是公家事，都是一種緣分。遇到了，有這個機會了，就應該珍惜。

Today many people don't like doing small things, meanwhile they are not able to do big things, and as a result, they achieve nothing. In fact, things, whether small or big, inside or outside the family, personal or public, are all causes and conditions. Since you've met it, having this opportunity, you should treasure it.

   365 Days Of Blessings

佛為什麼讓我們不為自己，要為眾生？這是佛心疼我們，慈悲我們。佛不會讓我們受苦、受累，而是讓我們解脫，你要明白這個道理。

Why does the Buddha teach us not to live for ourselves, but for all beings? This is because he loves us dearly, and has compassion on us. The Buddha will help us attain liberation rather than have us to suffer the pain and tiredness. You should understand this truth.

佛法越修越簡單，越修佛離你越近，你真正修進去了，學進去了，佛性自現，自然光明。

The more you practice, the easier the Dharma becomes; the more you practice, the closer the Buddha approaches. When you are really practicing and learning Dharma, the Buddha nature appears itself, naturally and brilliantly.

我執我愛、自私自利讓我們的心量特別小，什麼也容納不了。當我們發出慈悲心、菩提心了，心胸打開了，一切都能圓融了，才是解脫。就是要放下「我」，看破「我」，知道「我」的不存在。

Self-attachment, self-love and selfishness make our mind narrower, capable of accommodating nothing. Only when we arouse compassion and bodhichitta, our mind is opened up, and we can harmonize everything, that is liberation. What we should do is to let go of "self", see through "self", know the inexistence of "self".

365天的加持

慈 悲心就是一種清
淨的愛。

*Compassion is a kind
of pure love.*

把「我」看淡了，才能放下「我」；放下「我」了，才能真正為眾生；真正為眾生了，才能得到解脫。

Only by regarding "self" as unimportant, can we cast off "self"; only by casting off "self", can we really live for all beings; only by really living for the beings, can we attain liberation.

我們就是太在乎別人的看法與想法了，所以總是活在別人的目光下，在患得患失中煩惱痛苦。

We do too care about other people's opinions and thoughts, so we always live under others' eyes, being annoyed and suffering from the worry of gain and loss.

十月二十一日　　21st, October

問題不在別人身上，在自己的身上。自己一轉，什麼都會轉；自己一變，什麼都會變。在這個圈子裡轉不過來，這是問題。

The problem isn't in others, but in self. When self turns, everything turns; when self changes, everything changes. You cannot break through this circle, this is the problem.

十月二十二日　　　　*22nd, October*

功德是積來的，福報是修來的。想發財，想積累財富，就多布施，從心裡捨。有這個捨心，財富自然而然就有。

Merits come from accumulation, blessings come from practice. If you want to make a fortune and accumulate wealth, you'd better give more from the heart. With the generous mind, wealth comes naturally.

有佛法就有辦法，不用着急，沒什麼可怕的，一切都能解決！我們都是信心不足，一遇到困難、違緣、障礙，就手忙腳亂的，做不到一心念佛。

There is Dharma, there is a way. Don't be worried. It's nothing horrible, and everything can be solved. We all lack faith. When we face difficulties, obstacles and barriers, we are hurry-scurry, not being able to chant Buddha's name wholeheartedly.

從聞法中得到的智慧叫聞慧，從思維中得到的智慧叫思慧，從修行中得到的智慧叫修慧。沒有聞慧不會有思慧，沒有思慧不會有修慧。這都是有次第、有因果關係的。

The wisdom from listening, reflecting and practicing is called wisdom of listening, reflecting and practicing respectively. Without wisdom of listening, there's no wisdom of reflecting, without which there will not be wisdom of practicing either. There is sequence and causality among them.

發菩提心，行菩薩道，要從自己身邊有緣的眾生做起。無緣的眾生想度也度不了。

To arouse bodhichitta and to practice the Bodhisattva teachings, we should start from the destined beings around us. We could not save the beings without connections with us even if we wish to do so.

學佛首先要明理。我們是要學佛的，不是要學魔的。你迷了，就是魔，迷着做事情就是學魔；佛是覺，你覺了，叫學佛。

The first step to learn Buddhism is to understand the doctrines. Whom we should learn from is Buddha but not Mara. If you are deluded, it is Mara, doing things in delusion is learning from Mara; Buddha is awakening. If you are awakened, it is called learning from Buddha.

佛法是恆順年代，恆順地區，恆順眾生的。知道自己處在何種年代、何種地區，正在面對何種眾生，這是智慧。這樣才不會有壓力，不會有障礙！

Buddhism is adaptable to all times, all areas and all beings. Knowing what time and area you are in and what kind of beings you are facing, that is wisdom. Only like this will you have no pressures or obstacles.

認認真真、老老實實地做一切事，修一切法，這才是真正的修行。

*D*o everything and practice all Dharma truly and seriously, this is the real practice.

去執着，去追求，也沒有用，不該得的東西肯定得不到；拒絕、不接受，也沒有用，該接受的一定要接受。

You can never get what you do not deserve even though you pursue or obsess with it; you have to accept what you deserve even if you refuse or are unwilling to accept it.

大乘佛法能圓融一切，容納一切，所以大乘佛法裡的解脫是究竟的解脫，大乘佛法裡的成就是圓滿的成就。

Mahayana Buddhism can combine and accommodate everything, thus the liberation in Mahayana is ultimate and the accomplishment in Mahayana is consummate.

365 Days Of Blessings

無分別的愛叫慈悲心。有慈悲心就不會有壓力，你可以輕鬆、快樂地過日子；沒有慈悲心，就得不到安寧，得不到真正的快樂和幸福。

The indiscriminating love is called compassion. With compassion you will have no pressure and live your life easily and happily; without compassion you will have no peace nor can you have real joy and happiness.

365天的加持

我們真正能夠為眾生了，就解脫了；我們真正能夠饒益眾生了，就快樂了。

If we are able to serve the beings whole-heartedly, we will be liberated; if we are able to benefit the beings effectively, we will be delighted.

做不到還非要做，這是一種罪過；能做到卻不去做，這也是一種罪過。做自己能做到的，才是正法，才是修行，才可以成就。

It is a sin if you insist on doing what you are not able to perform; it is also a sin if you refuse to do what you are capable of. Do what you can, this is the true Dharma, true practice, and will lead you to accomplishment.

想開一點，好不可能永遠好，壞也不能永遠壞，都會變。主要是自己的心，想明白了，想開了，就是聰明，就是智慧，就是解脫。

Think broadmindedly, both the good and the bad cannot last forever, and all will change. The matter of importance is your mind, as long as you can think it through, then that is cleverness, wisdom, and liberation.

我們現在為什麼覺得太累、太苦了？因為我們的心靈就像個流浪的孩子，沒有找到歸宿。本覺、本性是心靈的歸宿。我們學佛修行就是尋找心靈的歸宿，把心放回那個歸宿，把心安住於本覺當中。

How come we are now feeling too tired and too suffered? It is because our minds are just like wandering kids failing to find the home. The primordial nature, or the primal awareness, is the home of our mind. The purpose of our practice is to find that home, get the mind back to it, and abide the mind in the primal awareness.

有解脫的心，才能談為眾生。要有這個決心：輪迴太苦了，一定要脫離。在這個基礎上，才能發慈悲心和菩提心。

Only with a mind seeking for liberation, can we talk about benefiting the beings. We should resolve like this: samsara is so suffering that we must break away from it. Only on this basis can we arouse compassion and bodhichitta.

365 Days Of Blessings

佛法是解脫的方法，是解決問題的方法。如果你學佛修行了，增加壓力，增加煩惱了，就不是佛法，是邪法了。

Dharma is the path for liberation, the way to solve problems. If the practice of Dharma has increased your pressure and affliction, it is already not Dharma but an evil way.

一切法的本性都是緣起，沒有恆常的，都在剎那間變。緣聚緣散，緣來緣去，不拒絕，也不追求，一切順其自然。

The nature of all phenomena is dependent origination, nothing is permanent, and all are changing from time to time. The conditions gather and disperse, come and go. Do not refuse, do not pursue, let it be.

一個壇城裡，師徒之間、道友之間沒有矛盾衝突，能夠和睦相處，這是一種力量。有了這樣的力量，其它任何魔障都障礙不了我們。

In a Mandala, if there are no conflicts between the Guru and disciples, or the companion practitioners, and everybody lives harmoniously with each other, that is a kind of power. With such power, no negative forces can obstruct us.

365天的加持

能夠沒有自私自利，沒有要求、不求回報地去關心照顧他人，這就是為眾生，就是饒益眾生。

Whenever you do not have selfishness and can take care of others without demanding or expecting rewards, then you are serving and benefiting the beings.

怎樣念佛才能打掉妄念？真正弄明白了一切法的真相和真理，才能打掉妄念，打掉執着。

How to get rid of the distracting thoughts while chanting Buddha names? Only when you have really understood the truth of all phenomena are you able to get rid of the distracting thoughts and the attachments.

把「佛」字的含義弄明白了，這是一種正知正見；然後從心裡念佛，把心安住在這個正知正見上，自然而然就不會有邪知邪見了，也不會有妄念了。

Truly understanding the meaning of "Buddha" is a right view; then chant Buddha names from the heart while abiding the mind in such right view, automatically there will be no wrong views arising, nor the deluded thoughts.

 *365 Days Of Blessings*

315

念 觀世音菩薩是念一切諸佛菩薩的慈悲；念地藏菩薩是念一切諸佛菩薩的願力；念文殊菩薩是念一切諸佛菩薩的智慧；念一尊佛就是念一切佛，念一切佛也是念一尊佛。

Memorizing Bodhisttava Avalokitesvara is to memorize the compassion of all Buddhas and Bodhisttavas; memorizing Bodhisttava Kshitigarbha is to memorize the aspiration of all Buddhas and Bodhisttavas; memorizing Bodhisttava Manjusri is to memorize the wisdom of all Buddhas and Bodhisttavas; memorizing one Buddha is the same as memorizing all Buddhas, and vise versa.

修行不是一朝一夕的事，一定要堅持；尤其是在面臨諸多障礙和干擾時，更要堅持。

You must be persevering in your practice, since it will not be completed overnight; especially when facing a number of obstructions and disturbances, you need to persevere even harder.

顯密之間沒有衝突和矛盾，都是救度眾生脫離痛苦的方法。如果認為有矛盾和衝突，是個人的問題，不是佛法的問題。

There are no contradictions between Exoteric Buddhism and Esoteric Buddhism, both of which are means to liberate sentient beings from samsara. The thought holding there are conflicts is a problem of some specific individuals, rather than a problem of Dharma.

365天的加持

一切都觀為圓滿了，這樣的修行才不會造業，才不受因果，才可以超出輪迴。

Only when you are seeing all as perfect while practicing, will you not create karma, be out of the cause and effect, and finally break away from samsara.

相續中沒有生起出離心之前，無論修什麼法，念哪尊佛，怎樣精進，也不能成為解脫、成佛的因緣，都逃不出三界輪迴。

Before renunciation arises in your continuity, no matter what Dharma gate you practice, which Buddha name you chant, and how diligently you practice, none of these can become the cause for you to get liberation and attain Buddhahood, nor can you escape from samsara.

365天的加持

在修行的過程中我
們會遇到很多魔
障，但是，真正的對
境和敵人是自己的煩
惱、習氣。

We will encounter many negative forces during the process of our practice. However, the genuine objects and enemies are our own afflictions and habits.

人身是最難得的，生命是最容易失去的。我們一定要珍惜寶貴難得的人身，好好地利用它來承辦自己和一切眾生生生世世的利益！

Getting human life is the hardest while losing it is the easiest. We must cherish the rare and precious human life, through which to realize the interests of ourselves and other beings in all the lifetimes.

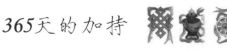

365天的加持

心淨，土淨。沒有清淨心，哪有清淨剎土？

As long as the mind is pure, the land is pure. Without a pure mind, where can you find a pure land?

有魔才有佛，你把魔看透了，它就是佛，這都是自己的心！你把他看成魔，他就是你的魔；你把他看成佛，他就是你的佛。

No Mara, no Buddha. If you can see the Mara through, then it is actually the Buddha, all is your own mind! If you regard it as Mara, then it is your Mara; if you regard it as Buddha, then it is your Buddha.

不管面對何種事情、何種現象，心永遠那麼平靜，那麼清淨，這叫解脫。

If your mind can always maintain calm and pure no matter facing what kind of issue or phenomenon, this is called liberation.

身累不是累，心累才是累；身苦不是苦，心苦才是苦。

The tiredness on body is not a tiredness compared to the tiredness on mind; the suffering on body is not a suffering compared to the suffering on mind.

輪迴比火坑厲害：在火坑裡你只會失去一次生命，在輪迴裡你要失去無數次生命；在火坑裡你只要感受幾分鐘的痛苦，在輪迴裡你要感受無量劫的痛苦。

Samsara is more terrible than a fiery pit: in a fiery pit you will just lose one life while in samsara you will lose numerous lives; in a fiery pit you will just suffer for several minutes while in samsara you will suffer for numerous kalpas.

365 Days Of Blessings

如果想擺脫輪迴、脫離痛苦，就不要怨恨別人，心甘情願地承擔、接受一切，當所有的怨都了結了，就不用再輪迴了！

If you want to escape from samsara and break away from pains, you should hold no grudge against others but willingly undertake and accept everything, once all enmities have been cleared, you are out of samsara.

沒有壞事，都是好
事。有病了，好
事！破財了，好事！
頭痛了，好事！沒有
智慧的時候你悟不
到。

Nothing is bad, all are good. Getting sick, good! Losing money, good! Headache, good! Without wisdom you cannot realize this.

上師是父親，壇城是母親，弟子是兒女，生生世世都是一家人。金剛道友必須要互相尊重，互相幫助，互相團結，珍惜這個緣分。

The Guru is the father, the Mandala is the mother, the disciples are the daughters and sons, and all are of the same family for all lives. Vajra brothers must respect each other, help each other, unite each other, and cherish this connection.

解脫不難，成佛不難。難在不相信——不相信佛法、不相信上師、不相信自己。懷疑是最大的障礙，不要製造障礙。

Getting liberation and obtaining Buddhahood is not difficult. The thing difficult is lack of confidence ----no confidence in Dharma, no confidence in the Guru, no confidence in self. Doubt is the biggest obstacle, do not create obstacles.

如果沒有破除我執，沒有去掉我愛，就不是真心，都是假的，都是自私自利，這樣永遠得不到真正的回報。

Before eliminating self-attachment and self-love, there is no true heart, each thought is fake and selfish, and like this you can never get the real return.

十一月二十九日 　　*29th, November*

業障不是本性，可以去掉，如同天上的雲，可以散掉。

Karmic obstacles are not primordial which can be eliminated, just like the clouds in the sky, which can disperse.

365 Days Of Blessings

333

積財做富翁不難！掌權做官員不難！得人身，尤其是得到暇滿的人身難！非常難！不是一般的難！

Accumulating wealth to become rich is not difficult! Obtaining power to become officials is not difficult! However, getting a human life, especially a life endowed with all the freedoms and advantages, is difficult! Extremely difficult! Even more difficult than what you can imagine!

365天的加持

把上師當作真正的如意寶，好好地珍惜他，真心地依賴他，虔誠地信任他，他能為你安排一切，能給你一切。

Regard the Guru as the real wish-granting jewel, cherish him wholeheartedly, rely on him seriously, trust him religiously, he will arrange and provide you everything.

記住：念千萬咒語不如祈禱一遍上師。上師是一切功德與加持的來源，要想功德圓滿，必須得到上師的加持。

Keep in mind: reciting the mantra thousands of times can not compare with praying to the Guru just once. The Guru is the source of all merits and blessings. To complete the merits, you must have the blessings from the Guru.

365天的加持

除了自己的家，哪裡有西方極樂世界呢？心清淨了，土就清淨。不用從自己的家裡走出一步，就往生到西方極樂世界了。

Except for your own home, where can you find another home of Western Pure Land of Ultimate Bliss? As long as the mind is purified, the land is purified. No need to walk out a single step from your home, you have already transferred to the home of Western Pure Land of Ultimate Bliss.

 *365 Days Of Blessings*

讓你的心不追隨過去、不迎接未來、不執着現在的時候，它自然就停了。就像風刮的沙，風一停，沙自然就落下來一樣。

Keep your mind from following the past, pursuing the future and attaching to present, then it will automatically stop. Just like the sand blew by the wind, whenever the wind stops, the sand automatically drops.

黃金和牛糞沒有區別，淨土和娑婆世界沒有區別，解脫和輪迴沒有區別，佛和凡夫沒有區別。那個時候才有平等心，有平等心才有清淨心。

No difference between gold and cow dung, no difference between the Pure Land and the Saha world, no difference between liberation and samsara, no difference between the Buddha and the ordinary. Only in that state can we have the mind of impartiality, and only with the impartiality can there be purified perception.

 *365 Days Of Blessings*

修上師瑜伽，最好是上師怎麼做你也怎麼做，上師怎麼說你也怎麼說，上師怎麼想你也怎麼想。慢慢地你的身口意就和上師的身口意相應了。

To practice Guru Yoga, you'd better follow how the Guru acts, speaks and thinks. Gradually your body, speech and mind will correspond to those of the Guru.

所謂的親仇、愛恨，都來自於我們的分別心。以三世因果的智慧來看待身邊的一切眾生，這個心態就是舍無量心，這是一種平等心。

The so called love and hatred all come from our conceptual thoughts. Treat the beings around us with the wisdom of causality spanning the three periods, such mind is the boundless impartiality, which is a mind of equality.

365 Days Of Blessings

業障深重不怕！當我們的相續中真正能夠產生菩提心的時候，無論多麼深重的業障都會立即消失，無論多麼淺薄的福報都會立即增長。

It is not terrible how serious your bad karma is! When bodhichitta really arises in our continuity, the bad karma, no matter how heavy it is, will disappear promptly; and the fortune, no matter how thin it is, will increase immediately.

很多人都把持戒當成痛苦了，都害怕持戒。如果不解脫，就要墮落惡趣感受痛苦，這才是真正要害怕的地方。該害怕的時候不害怕，不該害怕的時候卻害怕，這叫愚癡、顛倒。

Many people treat observance of percepts as a pain, and are afraid of keeping the vows. Actually, what one should really fear about is unable to get liberated and then fall into the lower realms suffering pains. Not fearing what to be feared about while fearing what not to be feared about, this is called ignorant or doing the reverse.

你真正能夠持戒了，才能身心清淨；身心清淨了，才能快樂、自在。這是脫離痛苦的方法。

Only when you can really observe the percepts, can your body and mind be pure; only with pure body and mind, can you feel happy and easy. This is the way to get rid of pains.

如果你有講經說法的能力，就一定要把這個能力布施給眾生；如果你沒有這個能力，就一定要為眾生好好地聞思修行。這就是法布施。

If you have the ability to give Dharma teaching, you must give this ability to all beings; if not, then you must learn and practice Buddhism for the interests of all beings. This is Dharma giving.

365 Days Of Blessings

如果有要求，有條件，要回報，就不是真正的布施，也不是真正的饒益眾生，更不是真正的菩薩心、菩薩行。

The giving with demands, conditions or expectations is not the real charity, nor the real benefit to others, nor any of the real Bodhisattva minds or acts.

沒有發心，僅僅有行為，不是真正的修行。

Without aspiration, the action itself is not the real practice.

修忍辱難，尤其是在對境中修忍辱非常難。如果真正能在對境中修成了忍辱，這個功德是不可思議的！

It is hard to practice patience, especially when facing certain objects. If you can successfully complete the practice of patience under such circumstance, the merit so generated is unimaginable.

如果修行不精進，就說明了我們的出離心還沒有修出來。如果我們真正知道死神在一旁虎視眈眈地注視着我們，我們還能呼呼大睡，懈怠懶惰，得過且過嗎？

If we are not diligent in practice, it means we have not generated renunciation. If we really understand that the god of death has been staring at us alongside, can we still sleep soundly, drift along and keep on being indolent and lazy?

 *365 Days Of Blessings*

物質的享受不是真正的享受，精神的享受才是真正的享受；表面的快樂不是真正的快樂，內心的快樂才是真正的快樂。

The real enjoyment is spiritual rather than material; the true happiness is indwelling rather than superficial.

很多人不識字，沒有文化，卻成就了。原因是他一心一意，深信不疑，所以能得到加持。我們有文化，能看，能讀，但是到現在還沒有成就。原因是我們總懷疑，信心沒有到位。

Many people are illiterate but they finally get accomplished. The reason is that they are wholehearted and have firm faith without any doubt, thus they can get the blessings. We are literate, being able to read and write, however, we have not got realization until now. The reason is we always have doubts and our faith is yet to be in place.

 *365 Days Of Blessings*

佛覺，沒有煩惱，只有清淨心，所以他的境界是涅槃，是淨土；凡夫迷，只有煩惱，沒有清淨心，所以他的境界是輪迴，是娑婆世界。

The Buddha is awakened, having no affliction but pure mind, therefore his realm is nirvana, or pure land. The ordinary is deluded, having no pure mind but affliction, therefore his realm is samsara, or the Saha world.

365天的加持

放下是放下妄想和執着，而不是放棄責任和義務。

Letting go is to let go of illusion and attachment, rather than to give up the responsibility and obligation.

凡夫沒有一心念佛，有好和壞的分別，有佛和魔的分別；有時候執着佛，有時候執着魔，實際上佛和魔都是因自己的執着而顯現的。

The ordinary people are not chanting Buddha names wholeheartedly, discriminating good and bad, Buddha and Mara: sometimes they are attached to the Buddha, sometimes to Mara, not knowing that Buddha or Mara is just the reflection of their own attachments.

有分別念，有妄念，所以有壞人、壞事，有不好的地方。一旦遇到這些的時候，心裡就特別煩惱、痛苦，就又開始了輪迴。

Due to the existence of conceptual thoughts and delusion, there are evil people, evil things, and bad places, whenever encountering these, one will suffer serious annoyance and pains, and then the samsara continues.

 *365 Days Of Blessings*

有和就有安樂，就有幸福。一個家庭和諧，這個家庭就會幸福美滿；一個單位和諧，這個單位就會穩定發展；一個國家和諧，這個國家就會強大昌盛；整個宇宙和諧，就會到處充滿和平、安樂、祥和。

Whenever there is harmony, there is ease and joy. A family with harmony will become blissful and happy; a company with harmony will develop smoothly; a country with harmony will turn strong and prosperous; the universe with harmony will be replete with peace, comfort and serenity.

365天的加持

眾生是累生累世的父母，我們怎能念父母的過錯？

The beings have been our parents through lives, how can we mind the parents' faults?

 365 Days Of Blessings

如果在吃喝玩樂中度過人生，和動物沒有區別，這叫虛度。學佛修行、解脫成佛，才是其他眾生做不到的。

If we spend our life in eating, drinking and enjoying, we are no difference with animals, this is called misuse. Only practicing Dharma and attaining Buddhahood is what other beings cannot do.

釋迦牟尼佛也沒能擋住世人造口業，我們能擋住嗎？別人愛怎樣說就怎樣說，愛怎樣看就怎樣看，自己有正確的目標和方法就行，能下決心，有信心，一定能成就。

Even the Buddha Sakyamuni could not prevent people from creating speech karma, can we make it? No matter how other people prefer to talk and think, as long as we have the right goal and path, have confidence and be able to resolve, we will surely accomplish.

修行就是用佛法活着，用佛法面對事情，用佛法解決問題。

Practice is to live with Dharma, face and resolve issues with Dharma.

為 度眾生要成佛！
真正從心裡發出
這樣的誓願，上師三
寶每時每刻都會關照
你，加持你；善神護
法每分每秒都會圍繞
你，護持你。你的一
切、一切會越來越圓
滿，越來越吉祥。

To attain Buddhahood for the liberation of all beings! When you really have made such aspiration from your mind, the Guru and the Three Jewels will take care of you and bless you at every moment; the virtuous deities and Dharma protectors will surround and protect you at all times. Everything of you will become increasingly perfect and auspicious.

 *365 Days Of Blessings*

佛菩薩是沒有分別的，但他們度化眾生時，不是攝受所有的眾生，而是攝受有緣的眾生。家人、親朋好友是與我們最有緣分的眾生，關心、照顧他們，這樣生活、工作，才是真正的修行。

Buddhas and Bodhisttavas do not have conceptual thoughts, even though, while guiding the beings, they could only guide those who have connections with them but not all beings. Family members, relatives and friends are the beings most connected with us, care about and attend them, such way of living and working is the real practice.

365天的加持

觀音菩薩無處不在，到處都有，但是我們都不相信，有點事情就害怕了。如果真相信這個道理了，還用害怕嗎？

Bodhisttava Avalokitesvara is everywhere, but we don't believe in it, therefore will feel afraid whenever something comes. If we really believe in this truth, do we have to be afraid?

365 Days Of Blessings

不要輕易評說別人，這樣容易造業；不要輕易相信別人，這樣容易受騙，容易修偏走邪路。

Don't casually evaluate others, for it is easy to create karma; don't rashly trust others, for it is easy to be deceived, deviate from the right path and walk towards an evil way.

在日常的生活當中，把一切都做得圓滿又殊勝，才能法喜充滿，這才是有修行，才是佛，才是極樂世界。

In our daily life, only when everything is done perfectly and supremely, can we be filled with bliss of Dharma, only this is the real practice, the Buddha, and the Pure Land of Ultimate Bliss.

365 Days Of Blessings